Something from the Cellar

Something from the Cellar

More of This & That

Selected Essays from
the Colonial Williamsburg Journal

by

Ivor Noël Hume

Photography by David M. Doody
Additional photography by Tom Green, Hans Lorenz, Ivor Noël Hume,
and the staff of the Colonial Williamsburg Foundation

Colonial Williamsburg
The Colonial Williamsburg Foundation
Williamsburg, Virginia

© 2005 by The Colonial Williamsburg Foundation

20 19 18 17 16 15 14 13 12 11 10 09 08 07 06 05   1 2 3 4 5 6 7 8

Printed in Singapore

Library of Congress Cataloging-in-Publication Data

Noël Hume, Ivor.
   Something from the cellar : more of this & that : selected essays
from the Colonial Williamsburg journal / by Ivor Noël Hume ; photography by David M. Doody ; additional photography by Tom Green
. . . [et al].
    p. cm.
   ISBN-13: 978-0-87935-229-5 (pbk. : alk. paper)
   1. Tidewater (Va. : Region)—Antiquities. 2. Excavations (Archaeology)—Virginia—Tidewater (Region) 3. Tidewater (Va. : Region)
—History. 4. Archaeology and history—Virginia—Tidewater (Region)
5. British—Virginia—Tidewater (Region)—Antiquities. 6. Virginia
—Antiquities. 7. British—Virginia—Antiquities.   I. Colonial
Williamsburg Foundation. II. Title.
F232.T54N635 2005
975.5'1—dc22

                                                    2005018973

ISBN-13: 978-0-87935-229-5
ISBN-10: 0-87935-229-9

Book design by Helen M. Olds

Colonial Williamsburg is a registered trade name of
The Colonial Williamsburg Foundation, a not-for-profit
educational institution.

The Colonial Williamsburg Foundation
PO Box 1776
Williamsburg, VA 23187-1776
www.colonialwilliamsburg.org

Frontispiece: The author in a tight spot on the site of the John Custis House in Colonial Williamsburg's Historic Area. A fire at the John Custis House circa 1810 left behind only the cellar hole and this brick drain leading toward Francis Street.

CONTENTS

FOREWORD

Meet a gentleman who keeps his eyes open, a fellow who notices things, things most of us don't, Ivor Noël Hume. Not merely a person of vision—though he is that, too—but a man whose glance fastens on details the rest of us are likely to overlook and sees in them things we wouldn't, even if we didn't. Before you trouble to read that sentence again, an anecdote to make its meaning plain:

One early winter morning two colleagues stood chatting on a footpath outside the offices of *Colonial Williamsburg,* the popular history journal of the Colonial Williamsburg Foundation. They were putting off the moment they had to go to their desks and get about the business of the day, toeing their shoes in the sandy soil like two boys in a schoolyard waiting for the bell to ring, when up bustled Noël Hume. In his hand was his newest manuscript for the magazine, photos and illustrations included, ready for delivery to the editor inside, first thing that day.

He stopped in midstride, stooped, and began to pick shiny shards of something out of the dust at their feet. Rising, he held out his hand, on his palm a half-dozen bits of patinaed glass—semiturquoise clear, but subtly crazed with metallic reflections of blue and red and maybe green, fish-scale colors, colors that danced and shifted as he turned them in the low eastern light.

They were, Noël Hume said, fragments of window glass from a structure that, by deduction, must have stood on the lot about two centuries before. That he so readily spotted something of interest in what the two idlers had not regarded, and saw past the debris down two hundred years, is a lesson in the meaning of acuity.

To save you a trip to the dictionary, the definition is "sharpness of vision; the visual ability to resolve fine detail." Which well describes a person who can gaze at a shelf of chamber pots and see a story, as Noël Hume does in "Mentioning the Unmentionable," or who can consider a James River shoreline and see in what is *not* there something to write about, as he does in "Plimoth and the Rock of Ages." In "New Discovery at Martin's Hundred"—more or less an apology for an error that would have gone uncorrected by anyone but a writer of Noël Hume's respect for readers—he spots in the transcription of a document something even the transcriber missed, but which caught Noël Hume's eye, and added to our understanding of a curious corner of early America.

A newsmagazine introduced me to Noël Hume in 1979 when I was a thirty-something expatriate Virginian and news editor for the great gray Associated Press in Nashville, Tennessee. An immoderately enthusiastic review of his tenth book, *Martin's Hundred,* said—if I recall correctly—that Noël Hume was a self-trained archaeologist, now in charge of that department at the Colonial Williamsburg Foundation, and, by many lights, the inventor of the North America historical branch of that science. What that meant I didn't consider, or much care, but the article said he'd just finished fascinating work on a remarkable find on a Colonial Williamsburg plantation property. That led me to a bookstore, and a weekend's adventure in a reach of the past buried for 350 years, lately uncovered by Noël Hume.

The chapters detailed discoveries at the forgotten site of a 1620s settlement of Englishmen and -women sent to the New World by stockholders in the Virginia Company of London. From rows of round stains in the ground—postholes—Noël Hume comprehended the walls and rooms and roofs of homes, yards, barns, a storehouse, and two palisaded forts. Examining skeletons recovered from shallow graves, he deduced details of an Indian attack in 1622 that laid waste most of the Virginia colony. From a backfilled well, he comprehended a passage about the colonist's use and disuse of face-plated armor helmets in the New World wilderness. In a line of coffin nails, he saw something of the rituals of death in the cultural landscape of America that no one had observed since the seventeenth century.

Like most young writers, I flattered myself that I recognized a storyteller when I saw one, and Noël Hume sure could tell a story.

A year before, Noël Hume had contributed the first story to the first issue of *Colonial Williamsburg,* an article titled "Carter's Grove—An Archaeological Anniversary Present." Few issues of the magazine have since gone to press without a story bylined by Ivor Noël Hume, and every one of his contributions has been memorable for its intelligence, wit, and perception. Most of all, distinguished by his informed imagination, and his way with ideas, as well as words.

A dozen years passed before I had the chance to meet Noël Hume in person, and consider his talents at firsthand. I'd come into a speechwriting job with Colonial Williamsburg and was taking on the odd assignment from Wayne Barrett, the journal's editor. Barrett introduced us.

Barrett was also among the first people to see the potential appeal of a book of Noël Hume's journal stories and put together *In Search of This and That: Tales from an Archaeologist's Quest.* It has gone through three printings since its publication in 1996.

It was my good fortune to have an opportunity to contribute a little to that project, and a little more to this, the second collection of Noël Hume's journal articles. May you enjoy the reading of it as much as the magazine and its staff have delighted in the association with a gentleman who keeps his eyes open, a fellow who notices things that most of us don't.

Dennis Montgomery
Editor, *Colonial Williamsburg,*
the Journal of the
Colonial Williamsburg Foundation

PREFACE

The life of an archaeologist is one of bits and pieces—a sliver of this and a shard of that. This second volume of articles from *Colonial Williamsburg*, the Foundation's journal, is no less eclectic. Its cast of characters runs from ancient Egyptians and pirates on the High Seas to witches in bottles and ghosts in the Wythe House. Because archaeology has as much to do with things—artifacts—as it does with people, these pages look at two of Williamsburg's most commonly excavated objects, wine bottles and chamber pots.

Although Williamsburg was the first of America's historic places to be put under the archaeologist's microscope, other places no less important in their historical significance have subsequently benefited from similar attention. Whereas much of eighteenth-century Williamsburg survived to be returned to its colonial appearance, other sites were less fortunate. The Fortress of Louisbourg in Canada, whose central building was much larger and stronger than any in Virginia, was completely demolished by the British at the end of the French and Indian War. Located on Cape Breton Island and once the maritime gatekeeper to French Canada, Louisbourg has been completely rebuilt after years of archaeological and historical research.

America's most famous historic site—at least to those living north of the Mason-Dixon Line—is Plymouth, Massachusetts, of which little or nothing has been found, and no town restored or reconstructed. Nevertheless, the 1620 "Pilgrims" have their homes at nearby Plimoth Plantation, where the township lives again thanks to extensive historical research and archaeological data from other sites of the same period. Further north at the mouth of the Kennebec River in Maine is New England's twin to Virginia's 1607 Jamestown. Excavations at the Popham Colony's Fort St. George have been going on for several years, and, thanks to a surviving town plan of extraordinary accuracy, information being gained there is helping interpret Jamestown, for which no plan survives.

Maryland, too, has its archaeologically explored colonial settlement sites, the earliest being Lord Calvert's St. Mary's City of 1637, and further north on the South River is a little forgotten port with a grand name—London Town. All these historic sites have their unique stories to tell and I hope that, having been introduced to them on these pages, my readers will be inspired to visit them all. One site you won't want on the itinerary is Williamsboro in North Carolina, and you will discover why when you read that essay.

The names of such great Virginians as Jefferson, Washington, Patrick Henry, and the Georges Wythe and Mason are familiar to most of Williamsburg's modern visitors. But few of us realize that all that history was confined within a time frame of about eighty years—scarcely more than a latter-day lifetime. The story of Williamsburg's restoration is almost as long, and the lives of many of the people involved in its resurrection have contributed as much to its cultural, social, and even political history as did their illustrious colonial predecessors. It is only fitting, therefore, that they, too, should inhabit these pages.

Ivor Noël Hume
Spring 2005

ACKNOWLEDGMENTS

Every writer's nightmare is first trying to remember the names of everyone whose assistance he has enjoyed, and then to spell them correctly. Of course, there are always the people whose faces one remembers but whose names never registered. To all those faces, my thanks and apologies. As for the rest, it seems best to cite them as one does any cast, in order of appearance. First to enter were Big Bone Lick State Park naturalist Jonathan Barker and Karie Diethorn, chief curator, Independence National Historical Park in Philadelphia, followed Jeffrey P. Brain, director of the Fort St. George Project in Maine; next, Plimoth Plantation director Nancy Brennan and historian James Baker, followed by the leadership team at St. Mary's City: executive director Martin Sullivan, research director Henry Miller, public programs director Dorsey Bodeman, and communications director Susan Wilkinson. At London Town, archaeological director Al Luckenbach and the London Town Foundation's executive director Gregory Stiverson were unfailingly helpful and informative, as were Parks Canada field unit superintendent Carol Whitfield, cultural resources manager William O'Shea, senior archaeologist Andree Crepeau, and the Fortress of Louisbourg's retired archaeologist Bruce Fry. My thanks, too, to Phillip W. Evans and Lewis Almond Henderson for sharing their knowledge of Williamsboro, North Carolina, and archaeological conservator John Van Ness Dunton and his assistant, the late Sandy Morse, who were here when I joined the staff of Colonial Williamsburg in 1956–1957. Here, too, was Kathy Yates, who later married vice president James R. Short and provided me with pictures and treasured memories. Equally ready to help was "Nanny" Frank, widow of Ernest M. Frank, the Foundation's architectural director in the transitional, future-setting years of the late 1950s and 1960s.

For my story on witches and witch bottles, my thanks go across the "pond" to Lyzbeth Merrifield, widow of my old friend and colleague Ralph Merrifield, deputy curator of London's Guildhall Museum, and to John Allen, archaeological curator at the Exeter Museum in Devonshire. I am particularly indebted to the interpreter who risked the scorn of her colleagues by recounting her experiences in the Wythe House and also to Colonial Williamsburg curator Tanya Wilson for ensuring that we exercised proper curatorial procedures while in the building. My thanks also to the lifelong resident, the late Gertrude Deversa, whose idea the first volume was and who urged me to try again to convene the Wythe House ghosts, but to do it alone without a photographer on hand to capture the spectral moment.

It used to be said that one picture was worth a thousand words and that cameras do not lie. Nowadays, of course, with digitized images and computer wizardry available at the click of a mouse, that is no longer true. As you thumb through these pages, however, it will be immediately apparent that the illustrations are both genuine and the product of a remarkable talent. Colonial Williamsburg photographer David Doody has been my friend and companion on all my adventures from the roar of the Nova Scotia waves to the silence of the Wythe House at midnight. It would have been no fun without him.

The Peale Great Incognitum, sold in 1848, resurfaced in the Darmstadt Hessisches Landesmuseum in Germany 100 years later.

Author Noël Hume at Monticello examines the same mastodon bones that Jefferson added to his natural history collection.

The Great American Incognitum

One can imagine the words rolling from the lips of Thomas Jefferson and echoing in whispers around the walls of Monticello—the Great American Incognitum. It was not America's third president who coined the phrase, however. It came from artist-showman Rembrandt Peale. Jefferson's contribution to the epithet was the word "incognitum." "It" referred to a great unknown—not to the vast, yet-to-be-explored reaches of the American continent, but to a collection of enigmatic bones unearthed on the Ohio River at Big Bone Lick.

That the site was rich in big bones and big teeth had been known to the Indians for centuries, and

to French explorers since the 1740s. It came to the notice of the English in 1762 when Indians trading at Fort Pitt offered them a massive tooth and part of a tusk. The relics wound up in London in the hands of Benjamin Franklin. In the same year, explorer James Wright wrote to Philadelphia naturalist John Bartram telling him that Indians reported seeing "5 Entire Sceletons, with their heads All pointing towards Each other, And near together, supposed to have fallen at the same time." Wright's informants "Judged the Creature when Alive must have been the size of a small house."

The discoveries attracted the interest of the European scientific community. In 1768, Scottish

A re-created mastodon trapped in a morass at Big Bone Lick in Ohio, where bones of the Great American Incognitum were discovered in the eighteenth century.

surgeon William Hunter published in the Royal Society's *Philosophical Transactions* the paper "Observations on the Bones Commonly Supposed to be Elephant's Bones, Which Have Been Found Near the River Ohio, in America." He wrote: "If this animal was indeed carnivorous, which I believe cannot be doubted, though we may as philosophers regret it, as men we cannot but thank heaven that its whole generation is probably extinct."

In France, the naturalist Comte de Buffon embarked on a measuremental study of big bones found in Europe and concluded that all the past and present animals of the North American continent were smaller than those of Europe. Buffon, whose given and family names were Georges-Louis Leclerc, was a pioneering scholar and blindingly Gallic. In his forty-four volume *Historie Naturelle* he said that not only was native American animal life smaller and inferior to European but so were its people.

Jefferson disputed the idea in his *Notes on Virginia*, hoping to put his French friends in their place by proving that the American incognitum was bigger and better than any comparable alive or dead European behemoth. Commenting on his own listing of comparative mammal sizes in America and Europe, Jefferson asked

> why I insert the Mammoth, as if it still existed? I ask in return, why I should omit it, as if it did not exist? Such is the œconomy of nature, that no instance can be produced of her having permitted any one race of her animals to become extinct; of her having formed any link in her great work so weak as to be broken. To add to this, the traditionary testimony of the Indians, that this animal still exists in the northern and western parts of America, would be adding the light of a taper to that of the meridian sun.

To Jefferson's mind, "He may as well exist there now, as he did formerly where we find his bones." A member of the American Philosophical Society, the Reverend Nicholas Collin, said that "the vast Mahmot, is perhaps yet stalking through the western wilderness," a creature "to whom the elephant is but a calf."

Jefferson's disinclination to believe an animal could become extinct had much to do with the widespread belief that the world began Sunday, October 23, 4004 B.C., a date calculated from the Bible by Irish Archbishop James Ussher in 1650. Scientists were perplexed by the idea that bones could become fossilized in less than 6,000 years. No one had identified dinosaur bones or realized that there had been a reptilian age before that of the giant mammals—or that they were 150 million years apart. That men of science were beginning to wonder whether there might be something wrong about taking Genesis at face value meant the hitherto unthinkable was being thought.

In Scotland, mineralogist James Hutton concluded that rocks could be the product of volcanoes, stretching time far beyond contemporary understanding. Buffon recognized the similarities between man and apes, and, on the basis of experiments with the cooling rate of iron, figured that the planet should be at least 75,000 years old.

He was in touch with such younger French scholars as Georges Cuvier, whose study of fossil bones made him the father of paleontology, and Bernard-Germain-Etienne Lacépède, to whom Buffon wrote February 24, 1803:

You have possibly seen in our Philosophical transactions, that, before we had seen the account of that animal by M. Cuvier, we had found here some remains of an enormous animal incognitum . . . and that there are symptoms of its late and present existence.

Jefferson, now president, told Lacépède, "The route we are exploring will perhaps bring us further evidence of it." The practical and open-minded Jefferson was not ready to dismiss the possibility that in unexplored regions of the country there might yet live animals of supra-elephantine proportions.

The route mentioned was planned for Meriwether Lewis and William Clark and their Corps of Discovery. Their epic journey of 1804–6 west beyond the newly purchased Louisiana Territory to the Pacific is familiar. Less well known is Jefferson's instruction to stop by Big Bone Lick to gather more incognitum bones. In this, Lewis and Clark were not very successful, and such bones as they did retrieve were lost when their boat sank. In 1807, however, Clark returned and eventually delivered bones to Jefferson. The following year the president sent some to Lacépède in the belief that "the collection

Charles Willson Peale painted the scene of his own mastodon exhumation in New York, 1806–8. He brought the remains to his museum in Philadelphia.

of the remains of the animal incognitum of the Ohio (sometimes called the Mammoth) possessed by the Cabinet of Natural History at Paris, is not very copious."

The notion that the public should be able to see and admire the discoveries of scientists and travelers went back in England at least to the Johns Tradescant, father and son of the mid-1600s, whose Lambeth Musaeum Tradescantianum—now the Ashmolean Museum—was to be home, they said, "for anything that is strang."

The American painter Charles Willson Peale was a man after the Tradescants' hearts. In 1784 Peale opened in Philadelphia a museum of natural history, geology, portraits, sea shells, and all things wonderful. He housed his treasures at his home, but so quickly did the collection grow he moved it to the hall of the American Philosophical Society, and in 1802 to the second floor of the Pennsylvania State House—Independence Hall. Like the Tradescants, Peale asked travelers, farmers, scientists, and ships' captains around the globe to bring him anything new and amazing.

Just as the Tradescants' Ark had exhibited such wonders as a "A Copper Letter-case . . . with a letter in it, which was swallowed by a Woman, and found," so Peale's museum could offer black bugs "cast up" from the stomach of a Maryland lady. Although he would have been insulted if his museum were likened to a freak show, its five-legged cow with two tails, and its two-headed pig, appealed to rubes as much as his portraits of Revolutionary War heroes did to Philadelphia's intelligentsia.

To make a lasting impression, a museum needs an elephant. Peale had a stuffed bison, but bison were big without being jaw-saggingly marvelous. When he heard a farmer in Ulster County, New York, had discovered the bones of a complete incognitum, the prospect of bringing the creature to the new nation's cultural capital was irresistible.

In 1801, with enthusiastic support from Jeffer-

Portrait of the artist as a bone collector. Peale's last self-portrait in 1824 revealed curatorial pride in his incognitum bone.

son and practical help from the manpower and tools of the army. Peale salvaged bones of two mastodons from deep, mud-filled pits in the Hudson River Valley. His mechanical means of separating bones from sludge were recorded for posterity in his painting of the event, which remains the mandatory introductory illustration for histories of paleontology.

In the late eighteenth and early nineteenth centuries the terms "mammoth" and "mastodon" were used interchangeably. Both were giants and had tusks of spectacular length. Prolonged and careful study of their teeth would eventually separate one from the other. Indeed, it was the discovery of isolated teeth that first caused colonial Americans to wonder whence they came and whether their progeny might still be out there waiting to devour colonists courageous or rash enough to venture into the great unknown. The first such tooth was discovered on a Hudson bank early in the eighteenth century, and others were later recovered from Big Bone Lick, among them one said to have been brought home by Washington.

Study determined that mammoths, like elephants, had flat surfaces to molars designed to feed on grasses, whereas those of the mastodon had cones, or cusps, that enabled them to eat the coarser vegetation from tree branches. Later, when skeletal remains were compared, it was established that mammoths were larger, standing as much as fifteen feet tall; the mastodons no more than ten.

About the history of mammoths in general, we now know a great deal more than did Jefferson, in whose day the Electoral Museum at Dresden included a *cabinet d'ignorance,* a name still retained in the British Museum of Natural History's geological department. Much still belongs in such a cabinet, but we know, or *think* we know, that the first mammoths reached North America about 1.8 million years ago at the beginning of the Pleistocene Epoch, which included four Ice Ages. In the pause between two or more of them, giant animals from Asia crossed the shallow or dry Bering Strait to Alaska. Three varieties have been identified as living in the United States at the end of the last Ice Age about 17,000 years ago: the Columbian, the eastern "Jefferson's" mammoth, and belatedly the woolly mammoth, which never ventured below the

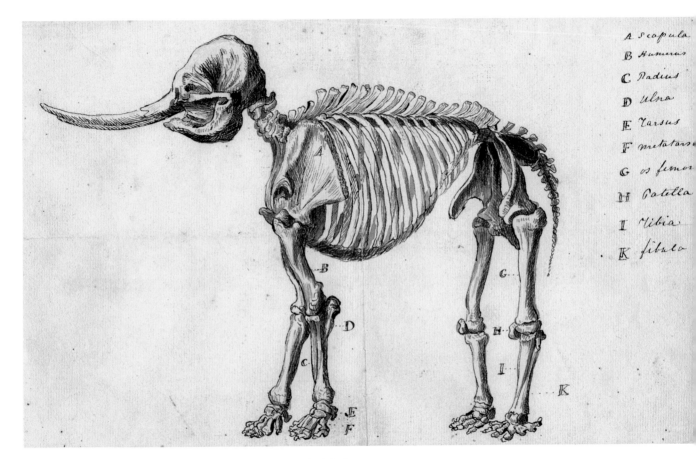

A scapula
B Humerus
C Radius
D Ulna
E Tarsus
F metatarso
G os femor
H Patella
I Tibia
K fibula

After concluding the tusks should point up, Rembrandt Peale sketched the beast.

ice fields. All were gone by about 10,000 B.C., leaving Jefferson and many neonaturalists and protopaleontologists to wonder why.

Today, Big Bone Lick on the Ohio River, south of Cincinnati, is a Kentucky state park able to show visitors the place where the story of American vertebrate paleontology was born, and where the black mud still grips the remains of animals so huge as to be beyond the imagination of colonial naturalists.

In any case, amid the patriotic fervor that followed the end of the Revolutionary War the notion of a giant new country epitomized by a giant old

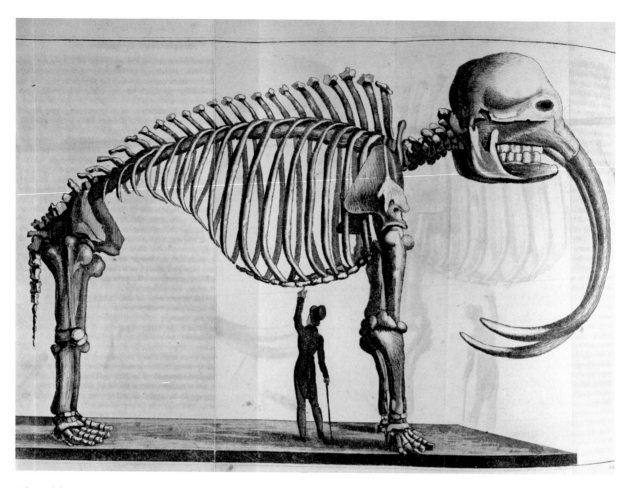

Edouard de Montulé drew the Peale mastodon skeleton in Philadelphia, still with incorrect down-curving tusks, in 1816.

mammoth made a splendid metaphor and a fitting victor over the declawed British lion. The national sensation resulting from Peale's recovery of his incognitum was fueled by his giving Philadelphia an eagerly anticipated Christmas present when, on December 24, 1801, he put the reconstructed goliath on show in his museum, with missing parts reconstructed by sculptor Benjamin Rush.

For hundreds of years the Old World mammoth had been a known, if not fully understood, reality. Skeletons found by Siberian hunters were a primary source of tusk ivory to be sold to European traders. Most of them came from the tundra, from which the ice had long since retreated, leaving the bones to be picked over by scavengers, animal and human. In 1799, however, a hunter named Schumachoff came upon a cliff-sized block of ice containing "a shapeless mass which did not resemble one of the great logs found in the river." When, three years later, he returned to the site, enough ice had melted to expose one side of a huge mammoth, its skin and hair preserved. The long mane on its neck, he said, was of coarse black hair while the fur on its body was a reddish brown. In 1805 Schumachoff freed the tusks and sold them to a St. Petersburg dealer. Two years later an English resident named Michael Adams heard about the discovery and organized an expedition to retrieve it. Schumachoff led him to the site, but they found the carcass destroyed by wolves, bears, and hunters, whose assorted footprints told their disappointing tale. The expedition gathered the bones—along with part of the hide that took ten men to carry to the boat. After they returned with it to St. Petersburg, the tusks were tracked down and reunited with the skeleton. Adams sold it to the city's zoological museum.

In Europe the Schumachoff mammoth outranked Peale's and evidently was recorded with greater accuracy. Besides, it had been found intact, whereas Peale's bones were parts of two animals.

Furthermore the Siberian specimen retained a piece of the hide that covered its skull. There is no knowing how soon, if ever, the Peale family saw an engraving of the St. Petersburg exhibit, but with bones from their second skeleton another exhibit was constructed and taken by Peale's sons Rembrandt and Rubens to London to show the Old World that America was not be outdone in behemothic bragging rights.

While in London the brothers Peale concluded that the tusks looked better pointing down—which they proceeded to make them do. Returning to Philadelphia late in 1803, Rembrandt Peale explained his reasoning to his father. Being a mastodon, whose crenellated teeth pointed to its having dined on stuff that was crunchy and chewy—in contrast to the cow-like mastication of a mammoth—it should be promoted as carnivorous and therefore an aggressive and dangerous creature ever ready to impale and scoop up its prey. The Peales may have been mindful of a New York physician, Dr. Samuel Latham Mitchell, who six years earlier told a Tammany Society audience how its namesake, the Indian Chief Tammannen, had fought with "alarming droves of mammoths, carnivorous animals, especially loving to feed upon human flesh."

Though Peale's excavated creatures had been found with their tusks curling upward, he agreed to turn them down. They were still in their scooping pose when French traveler Edouard de Montulé drew the skeleton in 1816.

Not only had Rembrandt Peale announced in England that his father's treasure was incorrectly assembled, but he said he believed the animals were extinct—this while Lewis and Clark were doing their president's bidding and keeping their eyes open for passing monsters. It seems likely, therefore, that relations between son and father were strained by these assertions.

Charles Willson Peale retired as head of his museum in 1810, leaving son Rubens as its administrative proprietor. Rembrandt wanted the job and was prepared to share it with his brother. Rubens, however, resisted the proposal, prompting Rembrandt to set about planning his own Peale Museum. In Baltimore. Neither he nor Rubens had been happy with the freak show ambience of the Philadelphia

museum. Once in control, Rubens got rid of most of the two-headed thises and thats and replaced them with biblical images more likely to appeal to the polite and pious. Meanwhile, Rembrandt commissioned architect Robert Cary Long Sr. to design and build in Baltimore what Rembrandt said was a "rendezvous with taste." When it opened in 1814, a star attraction was the skeletal remains of the second, "London" mastodon.

The artistic or tasteful ambience of the new museum was assured by the inclusion of panels depicting seminude females posed as painters, and his own *The Dream of Love,* which Rembrandt advertised as intended "to show the beauty, symmetry and grace of the female form." His father dismissed it as mere nudity and liable to get him in trouble with the Baltimore clergy.

In 1815, while Rubens was on vacation from the Philadelphia museum, his father returned to the curatorship and remained in joint control until he deeded the collection to his sons in 1820. At some date the family accepted the growing evidence that the tusks were mounted the wrong way and returned them to their original, less intimidating position. But up or down, mammoth mania was fading fast, and, by the time Charles Willson Peale died in 1827, declining ticket sales forced his sons to move the collection to less august, and cheaper, quarters in the Philadelphia Arcade.

In 1848, with bankruptcy looming, the family's Philadelphia no-longer-incognitum was sold to a foreign buyer. It would disappear for a hundred years before being rediscovered in the Hessisches Landesmuseum at Darmstadt in Germany, where it still resides. The rest of the collection, including teeth and bones from Big Bone Lick, were sold to P. T. Barnum, whose "museums" in Philadelphia, Baltimore, and New York were all destroyed by fire in the 1850s.

By the time his father died, Rembrandt Peale's rendezvous with taste had also run its course, and in 1829 his financial plight forced him to move out of the museum. The building had spoken to Baltimore's golden age of commercial and cultural ascendancy in the wake of the War of 1812. After Peale's departure, it became Baltimore's City Hall until 1878 before briefly serving as its first "colored" school. Thereafter it was put to several unpretentious purposes until 1930, when Baltimore historical preservationists decided that the building should be restored and reopened as the Peale Museum.

In the late 1920s and early 1930s, "restoration" mirrored the Colonial Williamsburg usage of the term, which allowed for demolition and virtual rebuilding. In the hands of architect John Henry Scarff, the building was taken apart and reborn in a form more grand and gracious. When the reconstructed Peale Museum opened in 1931, its exhibits bore scant resemblance to Charles Willson's or Rembrandt's cabinets of curiosities. In their place came fine Federal furniture, gilt-framed portraits, and gleaming silver. According to one report, visitors attending the reopening "were greeted with the strains of chamber music, the door held for them by footmen attired in period livery." Nevertheless, it was there that one had to go to see Charles Willson Peale's painting of the recovery of the Great American Incognitum.

But no longer. The museum closed in 1996 and three years later the painting and the rest of its collections, including the remaining mastodon bones, were transferred to the custody of the Maryland Historical Society.

Mastodon in the Denver Museum of Natural History, with prehistoric rhinoceros.

New Discovery at Martin's Hundred

The envelope was postmarked Salt Lake City—where I knew no one. The letter inside said, in effect, "I thought you might be interested to see the enclosed." I had read enough crime fiction to know that the next line should read: ". . . and I've kept the negatives." The writer's enclosure was indeed an embarrassment. It left little doubt that in my book and reports on Colonial Williamsburg's archaeological excavations at Martin's Hundred, I had made a horrible mistake—understandable, but a king-sized boo-boo just the same.

Many writers have compared archaeology to the work of police detectives who assemble clues to make their case; but there is one big difference. Had the Sergeant Fridays of law enforcement appeared in court and told juries that "we found fingerprints and a bloody knife, but, as we destroyed them, you'll just have to take our word for it that they were there," the problems of jail overcrowding long since would have been eliminated. Archaeologists, however, cannot avoid such apparent arrogance, because, as medieval alchemists used to say, "the art and mystery" of our investigations require that we destroy half our evidence as we go along.

Now and again, as in this case, new evidence turns up to prove that in archaeological terms we hanged the wrong man, and that is what has happened in Martin's Hundred at Carter's Grove. I hasten to add that the errors are not as devastating as the one suggested by my late wife, Audrey, who—more

Beyond the restored eighteenth-century garden of Carter's Grove, above, upper left, lies the still enigmatic outline of Wolstenholme Towne, destroyed in the great Indian attack of 1622. At the lower left of the aerial view can be seen the entrance and exit, close-up, left, for the Winthrop Rockefeller Archaeology Museum,* and in the center foreground lie the yet-to-be-excavated remains of another early eighteenth-century house.

*At the time of publication, the Winthrop Rockefeller Archaeology Museum and Carter's Grove were closed to visitation.—Ed.

as a cautionary exercise than in true belief—argued that perhaps we had not found Martin's Hundred at all but were digging on the neighboring plantation of the colony's secretary, George Sandys.

The unexpected letter came from genealogist William Thorndale, who had carefully transcribed from a recently available microfilm of hitherto unpublished Ferrar family papers two letters written at Martin's Hundred in 1625. The first he thought to be of only minor relevance, because it said little about life there. He had overlooked the significance of the two signatures: John Jackson, who identified himself as a bricklayer, and "Tho[mas] Ward pottmaker."

Here at last we had a name for the Martin's Hundred potter, and it was coupled with that of John Jackson, whose home site Audrey had equat-

ed with our Site B, where the now-famous locally made slipware dish dated 1631 was found. It was there, too, that the strangely shaped hole in the ground in which the dish was found was thought to have been a firing pit for a potter's kiln. My enthusiastic and grateful response to Bill Thorndale elicited an immediate reply that began: "Your letter of January 5 made me smile at the wonder of expertise. You found archeological implications in the 1625 Ward/Jackson letter that were totally opaque to me."

This, of course, happens to us all. One can read and reread the same documents a hundred times, but, without that little extra sliver of knowledge, significant information can slip right by us.

Writing in May 1625 to Nicholas Ferrar, their sponsor in London, Ward and Jackson bitterly

complained about the avaricious conduct of the hundred's governor, William Harwood, saying they had to give half their year's labor to him, and, that of their meager seven pounds' worth of tobacco, Harwood took six. Before leaving England, they had been told by Ferrar that each would be provided with two servants, but, when they arrived, they found that they had "not soe mutch as a foole to work with." They were not contented campers.

Some historians have assumed that once the remaining colonists had survived the Indian massacre of 1622, the danger had passed. This clearly was not so. Again complaining that Harwood refused to help them, newcomers Ward and Jackson declared that the ground allocated to them was so placed that "we can but one of us worke for the other of us must gard or ellse wee shall be in daunger to be

A newly discovered document describes a hitherto undetailed Indian attack on the Martin's Hundred plantation in 1623 and reveals graphic evidence of a wife's terror and a governor's cruelty as depicted in Vernon Wooten's illustration, above. It also suggests that the interpretation of an alleged pit-house excavated in 1976 was hopelessly wrong. The first interpretation assumed it to have been a one-room, below-ground structure, opposite, while the new evidence points to its having stood a story high above a deep cellar.

killd of the Indyanse." The two men signed themselves "your slavse in Virgenyae."

Bill Thorndale's second transcript was of a letter written a month later by another Martin's Hundred settler, Robert Addams; but it concerned events that had happened two years earlier. He described how, having built himself a house, on the day that "a woman servant of yours [Nicholas Ferrar's?] was slayne by the Indyans," he, Addams, was "assaulted by them" and took a bullet in his leg while the attackers destroyed his corn crop. Clearly, therefore, the Indians were no longer relying on their arrows but had become skilled in the use of the Englishmen's firearms.

The attack caught Addams's wife out in the open while he and his partner, Augustine Leak, were fighting to clear the area. She first ran "with much danger" to Governor Harwood and his people, "earnestly entreating their aid, but he out of too much feare and neglect would not stir out of the store where he was armed and guarded with your [Ferrar's] servants till the Indyans were fled." Instead, he "forsed her from them" and compelled her to flee on and to take shelter in a watch house, where she remained until the Indians had retreated.

Among the enduring mysteries of Martin's Hundred is the question of when Addams's wife arrived and what became of her. We do not even know her name, as she is not listed in any record of the living and dead in the hundred between 1623 and 1625. And, yet, we now know from Robert Addams's letter that she was there when the Indians attacked in the summer of 1623.

To historians the Addams letter says much about the character of Governor Harwood. But to the archaeologist, it means more. We now know that at the time of the 1623 attack, Harwood and his armed servants were holed up in a structure Addams described as a store. Of the seven buildings large and small we had identified as Harwood's home complex, only one fitted the description of a storehouse. As artist Richard Schlecht's rendering shows (page 10), we had interpreted it—based on the available archaeological evidence—as a solely subterranean structure covered by a thatched or bark-covered A-roof that reached, tentlike, to the ground.

It seems highly unlikely, however, that Harwood and his servants would have taken refuge in a building from which they could not see what was going on around them, and which, if the Indians had set the roof on fire, could have trapped and fried the lot of them.

It seems much more likely that the holes for massive posts found within the cellar actually supported an above-ground building erected by Harwood to serve as a defensible blockhouse on whose door the terrified Mistress Addams beat in vain. Until Bill Thorndale or another researcher trips over yet more evidence—and who dares say that they won't?—we have no documentation to tell when this building disappeared. Apparently it was gone when major changes were made to the Harwood site complex, for fragments of window lead found in debris dumped into the hole at that time are dated 1625. When, in February of the same year, a major Virginia census was taken, Harwood was still in charge at Martin's Hundred. He was listed as having three "houses," but no mention was made of a store.

The Addams letter demonstrates the fallibility of depending too heavily on negative documentary evidence. The store still had to be in existence when the census was taken, for Addams noted on June 16 that because the governor lived "in the midst of Mr. [Ellis] Emmerson and my selfe one each syde, so that Mr. Harwood, though your [Ferrar's] servants under his charge are but few, [he] may walke in safty from his house to ye store." This statement tells us not only that the store was still in existence, but that Addams and Emerson had their properties on either side of Harwood's—a highly relevant piece of information, for both of these postmassacre house sites still lie undetected beneath Carter's Grove acres.

The international interest generated by Martin's Hundred at the time of the excavations owed much to our finding the remains of the partially scalped, middle-aged woman we called "Granny." Following publication of the National Geographic article in which she was featured, scores of visitors to the site insisted on seeing the place where she had been found. That public interest—as well as the wording of the court order needed to disturb her—eventually led to her reburial in precisely the same spot, but this time she was afforded the dignity of

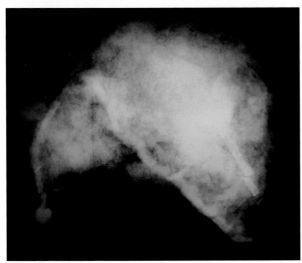

a handsome coffin and in it a sealed copy of the magazine to keep her company.

When we first found Granny, we discovered a badly decayed iron band looping over her right ear and bent back around the nape of her neck. The end by that ear terminated in a pewter knob; but the other ended in a twist of the iron strip, creating a loop where I had expected the matching knob to have been. I then interpreted the headband as a sometimes ornamental support for a hair roll of the kind worn by women of wealth and prominence, and in support cited the diary of Lady Ann Clifford, who, on May 12, 1617, wrote that on that day "I began to dress my head with a roll without wire."

Consequently, Granny was first identified as the slaughtered mistress of our Site H. Somewhat later, I discovered that wires and springs were used by women of all walks of life to hold lace and lawn caps in place. That knowledge, and also because Granny had been left where she died, led me to downgrade her from mistress to the "a maide" listed among the massacre victims. It remained my assumption that the length of the iron band had been shortened to fit her unusually small head and that the second pewter knob had been removed and replaced by the crude new terminal. I called it a "hand-me-down" kind of hair wire consistent with the attire of a maidservant.

The explanation left me uneasy, because a flat iron band cannot be bent as readily into a loop as can a round sectioned wire. Nor could it have adroitly been bent back from the crown of Granny's head to the back of her neck by a scalp-hungry Indian. But having no better explanation, I let it stand in the hope that nobody would challenge this interpretation.

It would remain uncontested for sixteen years, until Jamestown's archaeological curator Bly Straube

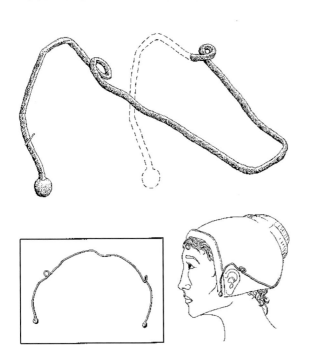

The woman the archaeologists called "Granny" had been wearing an iron spring to hold her cap in place. It is to be seen around her skull, top, and more clearly in the X-ray that shows the metal extending over her right ear and dipping around the nape of her neck. That configuration was at first thought to have resulted from Indian violence, and that in life the spring went over the crown of her head—as is seen in the line drawing, bottom left. It is now known to have followed the line shown in the larger drawing and represents a very different type of cap securer.

showed me an article written in Holland describing and illustrating several varieties of cap-securing wires used there in the seventeenth century. One of them passed up over the ears and looped around the nape of the neck, exactly as had Granny's. The loop I had interpreted as a replacement terminal was nothing of the sort. It was one of a pair, one on each side of the head, through which the band was pinned to the cap. Careful reexamination of the X ray of Granny's head made while the band was still in position revealed traces of a second, matching loop at the right side of the head, a detail that had gone unrecognized at the time and so was omitted from the reconstructed band now exhibited in the Winthrop Rockefeller Archaeology Museum at Carter's Grove.

Although these discoveries did nothing to further change our opinion about the person of Granny and how she died, the new evidence from Holland made sense, where before there had been only a nagging suspicion that something in my reasoning was wrong.

Among the many Martin's Hundred mysteries that still persisted, when the exhibits were installed in the museum in 1991, was the purpose of a small brass box discovered in the Site B potter's pit along with the 1631 dish. The box was lined with lead, and its punch-decorated hinged lid was secured with a delicate and fragile latch. The stamped ornament consisted primarily of rosettes, but among them was a single impression of a finger-pointing hand thought to be the city emblem of Antwerp.

Almost identical boxes had been found on the wreck of the *Batavia*, a Dutch East Indiaman that sank off the western coast of Australia in 1629, a date only two years earlier than our 1631 dish that served to date the box's context. In one of those from the *Batavia* were discovered several small squares of linen, which the finder thought might have been used as patches or wads to separate the charges from bullets used in early rifles. I was reluctant to accept that explanation, because the boxes are so delicate and their latches require such careful handling that neither would be appropriate for a shoot-or-get-shot rifleman or musketeer in the rough and tumble of battle.

Another similarly marked box had been found in the River Thames at London; but, more importantly, I also knew of one from an Indian site in upstate New York—and now in the Rochester Museum—that contained a flint. Years passed before I had the sense to put two and two together—or rather the flint with the *Batavia*'s linen patches. Was it possible, I wondered, that the linen was tinder and the flint a striker to ignite it? I turned to the source that provides the jumping-off point for any historical research—the *Oxford English Dictionary*. Under "tinder" it reads, "Any dry inflammable substance that readily takes fire from a spark and burns or smoulders; esp. that prepared from partially charred linen." Thus, the mystery boxes are mysterious no longer. They are tinderboxes, a necessity that few colonial households could do without—which raises another question: Why have so few been found?

As the result of excavations carried out between 1976 and 1981, Martin's Hundred returned to its place in Virginia history after sleeping through more than 330 years. Nevertheless, important questions still remain to be answered: Why were so many of the sites abandoned around 1640? Where are the home sites of Ellis Emerson and Robert Addams? What went on between about 1625 and 1710 on the partially excavated site that lies in front of the parking lot adjacent to the Carter's Grove reception center? Were the traces of an early eighteenth-century house discovered on the ridge west of the museum during its construction those of the original Carter and Burwell dwelling that preceded the mansion? And why are the Burwell tombstones located where there appear to be no graves?

That Martin's Hundred still retains many an undiscovered treasure as well as the answers to these unsolved mysteries is tremendously exciting and encouraging. But, alas, not so encouraging is the realization that I shall not be the one to find them.

late getting to Bath. Thermometer was 30 below in Bath this morning.

Lymans abutted the 1607 fort site. Hiram and Arthur were Stevens's sons.

With the homeward-bound *Gift of God* went a letter from Popham to King James assuring him that the local Native Americans thought the world of England's monarch and that his god was better than theirs. Popham said as well that they had told him that a great sea lay only seven days' march away, and, therefore, the long-sought, westerly passage to the riches of the Orient was almost in his grasp.

No record survives to show whether King James asked why, if the prize lay only a week's walk away, Popham had not put on his hiking boots and set out hot foot. But even if the king had written him such a letter, Popham would not have lived to read it.

When, in August 1608, Captain Davies returned to the Sagadahoc with his ship laden with supplies of food, arms, tools, and other necessary commodities, he found that, in spite of a winter described as "extreame unseasonable and frostie," the colony seemed in fair shape. But Popham and several of his settlers were dead, and the mercurial Admiral Gilbert had assumed the presidency. Davies also brought letters—letters whose contents would prove to be the colony's undoing. From them Gilbert learned that his elder brother, Sir John Gilbert, had died and left him a relatively rich man. His choice between remaining in the American wilderness or returning as lord of a Devonshire estate was quickly made, and, once his decision became known, the rest of the settlers began packing.

On October 1, Captain Davies's relief ship, with its stores still aboard, set sail with the little *Virginia* astern, together carrying the demoralized colonists back to England—leaving Fort St. George to vanish into the fog of history.

The English activity in Maine had been watched by the Spaniards with scarcely less concern than they had for the colonizing effort at Jamestown, far to the south. Although Spain had demonstrated its inability to land an army on the soil of England,

John Hunt's sketch of the Virginia *(detail), the first seagoing ship built by the English in America, will enable her to sail again in replica in time for the launching's 400th anniversary in 2007.*

its successes in the field of espionage would have impressed the KGB. Pedro de Zúñiga, the Spanish ambassador in London, had established a network of agents that reached into every aspect of Britain's foreign policy, from the royal court, to the Virginia companies, and, perhaps, into the Privy Council. Every document of interest to Spain seems to have been quickly copied and transmitted. Once scrutinized, they were passed to the Archivo General de Simancas, where they were carefully filed away—and forgotten. Among them was the then-unrecognized treasure that Captain Davies had carried to England in October 1607. It would remain there until the 1880s, when the United States ambassador to Spain, J. L. M. Curry, was shown a map at whose top were these words:

> The Draught of s^t Georges fort Erected by Captayne George Popham Esquier one the entry of the famous River of Sagadahock in virginia taken out by John Hunt the viiith day of October in the yeare of our Lorde. 1607.

Beneath it was a plan of the fort showing every important house, workshop, and fence—several delineated in post-by-post detail—each area numbered and supplied with the name of the occupant. It showed the placement of the artillery, the magazine, the church, and the storehouse.

We can assume that no matter their destination, colonizing expeditions sent from England were supplied with comparable instructions and development kits. Indeed, equipment lists attributed originally to Ralegh were reprinted in 1622 and again in 1630 to aid in the planning of an Anglo-French expedition to settle in what is now North Carolina. All in all, therefore, it seems reasonable to conclude that post-constructed buildings at Fort St. George would look pretty much like those built at Jamestown. But the map had a problem: It looked too good to be true.

Along with the twenty or so architecturally convincing and named buildings, John Hunt's plat showed them surrounded by a stone-laid defense work as formidable as any medieval castle's curtain walls—complete with cruciform arrow slots. Outside he drew a carefully bedded produce garden enclosed by a board fence supported by thirty-six elaborately finialed posts and exited through an arched gateway capped with something resembling a junior beauty pageant winner's tiara. Small wonder was it, therefore, that skeptics were ready to dismiss the Hunt plat as public relations nonsense.

The identity of Hunt himself was an unanswered question. Why was he entrusted with drawing the picture that was to be the company's prime tool in raising expectations and money for the successful continuance of the Popham project?

It fell to Jeffrey Brain, archaeologist for the Peabody Essex Museum of Salem, Massachusetts, to find a plausible answer. The sister of George Popham's nephew, Edward, who accompanied him to the Sagadahoc, was married to a John Hunt. Furthermore, Edward was married to the daughter of the military engineering draftsman Richard Bartlett. Thus, it seemed reasonable to conclude that John Hunt of Fort St. George learned his skills from Bartlett. While working on my 1994 book, *The Virginia Adventure,* and studying the evidence for the storehouse at Jamestown, I looked more carefully at the building Hunt had identified as ".5. the Store howse." He showed nine posts on a side, defining eight bays, and another between them at the end. As the spacing in Virginia is generally between eight and ten feet, a quick estimate suggested a building about seventy-six feet in length and twenty wide. But only archaeology could prove or disprove those proportions.

Over the years historians had promoted several locations as the site of Fort St. George, but of them Sabino Point made the most sense. Two test excavations there by the Maine State Parks Commission in 1962 and 1964 found no post holes but yielded a few artifacts, among them a fragment of a jar made in Devonshire and similar to others discovered on the 1609 wreck of the *Sea Venture* off Bermuda. The omens looked good, and, when Brain began more extensive excavations in the late 1990s, he found that postholes did exist. By the fall of 1999, he and his Maine State Museum field school had uncovered most of the storehouse and had proved the building had burned. But whether the fire was set by the departing colonists or later by the Indians no one yet knows—nor may they ever. As for my twenty foot width measurement, that turned out to be off by twelve inches. I fared less well, however, with my estimated length, which turned out to be truncated by one whole bay. The reason can only be guessed, but it is possible the settlers planned to extend the store when more supplies arrived in the spring of 1608, and that the departing Hunt knew it and drew accordingly.

With the accuracy of Hunt's drawing again questioned, Brain decided to find out whether the relative locations of other buildings to the store were similarly adrift. To do that he chose to look for the adjacent corner of ".3. the Admirals howse," which was shown with a chimney at one end, and appeared to be about five bays—approximately forty feet—distant.

The 1999 season's excavations located a corner of a building four and one-half bays from the storehouse, one that had a chimney at the end—the same position Hunt had shown on his drawing of the admiral's house. Artifacts found in its vicinity pointed to domestic occupation, and it was not hard to imagine that Raleigh Gilbert had lived up to his reputation as "a loose life" by smashing the German stoneware bottle whose fragment Brain discovered there. It called for no imagination on my part, however, to stand beside the storehouse excavation and watch the archaeologists lift the stub of one of the storehouse posts that Hunt had put to paper 392 years earlier.

Brain's excavations are to continue for years. But our hats are off to surveyor Hunt for having given that other Virginia its rightful place in the history of American architecture. In the meantime, a nonprofit foundation has been established to fund the building of a replica of the *Virginia* to be ready to put to sea in 2007—thereby commemorating the attempted settling of New England thirteen years ahead of the Massachusetts Pilgrims.

In 1607 ice and fog transformed pleasant summer into wintry misery—and still can, as this photograph shot in 1999 witnesses.

Plymouth Rock, above, may or may not have felt the feet of debarking Pilgrims. Reconstructed Plimoth village, left, in any case, could not have, but, near the original town site, it would be familiar to Miles Standish.

Plimoth and the Rock of Ages

The breathlessly eager, camera-ready tourist leaned over the rail of the Jamestown Ferry and asked, "Can you see the rock from here?" Her companion answered, "I don't believe so. I don't think it would be that big."

The exchange may be apocryphal. But it highlights the very real fact that the seventeenth-century history taught in the Plymouth Rock North had little to say about the first-permanent-English-settlement South. Conversely, students below the Mason-Dixon Line remember the *Mayflower's* descendants as Yankees who claim Plymouth, Massa-

chusetts, as the site of the first Thanksgiving when everybody knows that it was celebrated in 1617 at Berkeley Plantation in Virginia. Ironically, the North has a much better claim to another first, namely launching the first British ship built in America at Maine's Fort St. George in the summer of 1607. But allegiances being what they are, the event might have resonated better through time had the vessel been named the *Massachusetts* and not the *Virginia*.

I was raised in England, so my own historical education was markedly slanted toward New England and the *Mayflower's* buckle-hatted Pilgrims, about whom I remembered little other than that they prayed a lot, shot turkeys, and hanged witches. Of Jamestown, however, I recall absolutely nothing beyond a vague recollection of an Indian princess whose name was Poca-something—or maybe Minnehaha. But I was not alone in this. As recently as 1984, a Massachusetts historian was quoted as explaining to visitors that "smaller settlements in what was to become the United States also were active when the Pilgrims landed. They were St. Augustine in Spanish Florida, 1565; British Fort Nassau near Albany, 1614; and French Quebec, 1608." In short, ignorance of early American colonial history has by no means been limited to air-headed tourists on a James River ferry.

Not only were the Pilgrims thirteen years late in the founding settler sweepstakes, but their settlement has never been positively identified and in the minds of many remains as steadfastly lost as that of their Elizabethan predecessors on North Carolina's Roanoke Island. That the birthplace of New England culture and history should be memorialized by nothing more than a lump of rock inside an incredibly pretentious classical portico was an embarrassment made more pointed by the growing popularity of Colonial Williamsburg in the post–World War II years. Nevertheless, local New England pride in the Pilgrims and particularly in the annual celebration of Thanksgiving was much more venerable.

An "Old Colony Club" had been founded at Plymouth as long ago as 1769 and featured an annual dinner—with the inevitable speech. They called it Forefathers' Day to mark the anniversary of the Pilgrims' landing. Although the first national Thanksgiving is credited to the Continental Congress in 1777, it was President Abraham Lincoln who in 1863 put the celebration permanently on the American calendar. By then, interest in Forefathers' Day had languished and was destined to be absorbed into the national giving of thanks. Consequently, the need to revitalize the story of the 1620 settlers outside the stereotypical turkey feast became an issue planted firmly in the mind of young Bostonian Harry Hornblower, who in the late 1930s had been inspired by the restoration of several early Plymouth buildings in the Williamsburg manner.

In 1945, with the war over and a sunlit feel-good future ahead, Hornblower persuaded his father to donate $20,000 to Plymouth's existing Pilgrim Society for:

The erection of a Pilgrim and Indian Village, which would include not only replicas of Pilgrim houses and of Indian tepees, but also a museum where Indian relics might be displayed.

Like Pilgrims from the past, interpreters in seventeenth-century garb bring the Plimoth tableau alive.

Though the venues may be aboriginal in style, the artifacts they contain speak to cultures an ocean apart.

slipped again into half-forgotten history. There it remained until 1966, when the Maryland General Assembly established the St. Mary's City Commission and instructed Forman to prepare a plan for the site's development. This coincided with the State of Maryland purchasing a 900-acre tract on which part of the colonial capital had stood. The most intensely developed and archaeologically important acreage, however, remained in private hands, and not until 1980 did the state acquire another crucial 200 acres.

Orin Bullock, previously Colonial Williamsburg's director of architectural research, assisted Forman in the creation of a master plan. Four years later, the Foundation's current vice president for research, Cary Carson, would head the research effort, assisted by an archaeologist trained in Williamsburg. Consequently, Colonial Williamsburg has

long enjoyed a close relationship with her sister colonial capital to the north.

Even while St. Mary's archaeological renaissance was in its infancy, educationally oriented visitor attractions were being launched, among them the interpretation of the statehouse as a colonial court, and the building of a seagoing replica of the *Dove*. These, and a sample plantation house, provided a nucleus around which costumed interpreters reenacted typical moments in the lives of the settlers. That fledgling interpretive program owed much to experience previously gained by the staff of Plimoth Plantation, and before long the State of Maryland had a laudable venue wherein to tell its seventeenth-century story.

True to the idea of a proprietorship, in 1634 a hundred acres around the Calvert mansion had been named the Governor's Field but later was broken into subsections, one of them a three-acre tract named Smith's Townland. That land grant was secured in 1666 by one William Smith, whose lease required him to build on it an inn for "the Accommodation of the Country." That he did. The first operator of Smith's Ordinary was a Dutch immigrant named Garret von Sweringen, who ran it until 1677, when he moved to another nearby location and leased it to an Irishman named John Deery—who promptly died. Shortly thereafter fire broke out in the building and "consumed the same

An Indian longhouse and, beyond it, a lodge for the first colonists.

The newly reconstructed "Smith's Ordinary" is but one step in an ambitious interpretive program.

to ashes," thereby ending the short life of St. Mary's City's best recorded hostelry. It was not large by later colonial inn standards, measuring only 20' x 30', much of it taken up by a massive hooded fireplace that served as kitchen and a cozy nook for huddled ale swillers in winter.

The ordinary's ground plan, revealed by excavations supervised by research director Henry Miller, has been convincingly reconstructed under the watchful eye of architectural curator Eric Marr. But much of the credit for this important interpretive addition belonged to a team of housewrights from Plimoth Plantation who dressed the timbers in Massachusetts and erected them in Maryland.

Many house sites remain to be archaeologically explored and will one day be rebuilt, as will the chapel. In the meantime, based on Forman's and later surveys, the locations of the vanished structures are being marked by skeletal frameworks that demonstrate the extent of the old town as it was in the mid-1600s. Even now, Smith's Ordinary is but one of the reconstructed colonial buildings that give St. Mary's City its special ambience.

For this visitor, however, the Native American longhouse, with its white wolf pelt, authentically reproduced earthenwares, gourds, tools, and weapons, is the most evocative. It strikes a vivid contrast between the warm "togetherness" of aboriginal life and the austerity of the living quarters common to all but a few of Lord Baltimore's freedom seekers.

Tribal help enabled the Marylanders to get started in their new and strange environment, a point well made by another reconstructed hut built in native style and of the kind inhabited by English settlers until they had time to erect European housing. The cultural juxtaposition teaches that this amicable relationship between Calvert's people and the indigenous tribes set the early history of Maryland apart from the arrogant excesses of its Jamestown neighbors.

The Historic St. Mary's City Commission made it clear that the site was being resurrected to help modern Marylanders better appreciate their colonial heritage, and that is the interpretative aim. Most of the visitation is drawn from regional school groups, and, although the interpreters welcome all comers, no one frets that the buildings are not overrun. Indeed, that is St. Mary's City's greatest asset. Communing with its past is best achieved when little is heard but the lapping of the tide around the hull of the *Dove* or the cry of a departing heron. In retrospect, perhaps, architect Henry Forman was not so far off the mark when he called this beguiling place a city of romance.

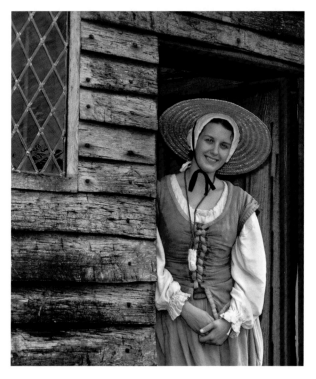

Completion of the reconstruction of St. Mary's City's tavern is a good reason for interpreters to smile.

Archaeologist Al Luckenbach pieces together the pottery and the story of London Town, a lost Maryland town that once was a busy tobacco port.

In Search of Lost Towns
A Maryland adventure

Losing one's car keys, one's eyeglasses, or even one's shirt is a concept easy to grasp, but losing towns takes negligence to a new level. Architect Henry Chandlee Forman coupled Maryland's St. Mary's City with Jamestown in his book *Jamestown and St. Mary's: Buried Cities of Romance*. Virginia has more lost settlements, though people have done little to find and explore them. That, however, is not true of the administrators of Maryland's Anne Arundel County, which has its own archaeological director and a staff to pursue its ambitious and successful Lost Towns Project. The centerpiece is the reemergent London Town, begun on the South River below Annapolis in 1683.

Funding archaeological projects is not an easy sell, but Anne Arundel County archaeologist Al Luckenbach has the Midas touch and has garnered gold from public funds and private donations that have kept the Lost Towns Project in high gear for many years, and it is likely to continue beyond his lifetime. Few states have been the equal of Maryland in its commitment to using its archaeological sites as tools in awakening students to the riches of state and local heritage. That is the driving force behind the Lost Towns Project, and it is manifested daily when schoolchildren sit wide-eyed as volunteer interpreters take them down into the cellar of Rumney's Tavern in London Town.

The centerpiece of Historic London Town, this circa 1764 building was the home, tavern, and business place of ferry operator William Brown.

From the town's name one might expect London to have been Maryland's premier city, but that distinction belonged to the largely Catholic St. Mary's City further down the coast. In 1649, Protestant Dissenters established their own settlement on the Severn River north of Annapolis and called it Providence. But providence did not favor it, and within little more than a generation the wood-built houses disappeared. In 1668, Governor Charles Calvert established eleven seaports "for the discharging and unloading of goods and merchandizes out of shipps & boates and other vessells," and fifteen years later the Maryland General Assembly incorporated several towns on the Chesapeake Bay, London among them. Each was to occupy a hundred acres to be divided into blocks of one-acre house lots separated by streets, most of which ran down to the water. And there was plenty of it, the town being bordered on three sides by waterways: Almshouse Creek, as it is called today, to the north; South River to the east; and Glebe Bay to the south. A busy port, it became the principal tobacco shipping point for that part of Maryland and the county seat from 1685 to 1695,

when the courthouse was moved to Annapolis.

London's aspirations to become a capital were thus dashed, and for twenty and more years the settlement rested on what remained of its laurels. But in the early eighteenth century, when Maryland tobacco exporting became big business, London Town grew and prospered again. Ships meant sailors and sailors needed refreshment, liquid and otherwise. Taverns were built to accommodate them, among them that of shipwright and ferry operator Edward Rumney.

The site of Edward Rumney's establishment has been found and excavated by Luckenbach's team, and its cellar is now kept open as a teaching aid. A vertical section through the filling graphically showed how silt and trash had accumulated within it, and proposals were made to preserve this picture of the past. But stabilizing dirt is difficult to achieve without distorting its appearance, and so a full-scale photograph of the soil capped by a reconstructed tavern floor became the solution—and a successful one. Among the artifacts recovered from the cellar were fragments of three English delftware plates decorated with a mermaid or merman figure borrowed from a Dutch tile design. Although nobody knows the name of Rumney's tavern, it seems possible, even likely, that it was identified by a mermaid-painted sign. True or not, the mermaid is today the promotional icon of the London Town Foundation, which owns or leases twenty-three acres of the once hundred-acre community.

In the spring of 2002, with guidance from Colonial Williamsburg architect Willie Graham, the London Town Foundation began the reconstruction of another of Luckenbach's excavated sites, one built on about 1690 and owned by David Mackelfish, who called himself "the Lord Mayor of London." Even more ambitious is to be the simultaneous construction of an archaeological museum and visitor center, which, like the Winthrop Rockefeller Archaeology Museum at Colonial Williamsburg's Carter's Grove, will be largely underground. This

Schoolchildren not only ask questions at London Town but help archaeologists sift soil in search of artifacts. As many as sixty children visit every Wednesday.

project, however, differs in that the subterranean building will be erected in an already existing hole in the ground—one provided by an abandoned, three-stories-deep water treatment plant. Part of the funding comes from the board of Anne Arundel County, more from private gifts and grants, and $2.5 million from the state's share of the National Transport Enhancement Funds program.

None of this would have come about had it not been for the existence of a lone brick building that had little to do with the posts-in-the-ground, or earth-fast, wooden buildings of London Town's heyday as a port. Built about 1764, when much of the old town had already rotted away, this was the handsome Palladian-style brick home, tavern, and place of business for one William Brown, who operated the lucrative ferry between London Town and Ferry Point on the Annapolis peninsula and on the overland route between Williamsburg and Philadelphia. In the remaining colonial years traffic was heavy and business brisk, but with the onset of the Revolution, coupled with falling tobacco prices and the decline of Williamsburg as a political and cultural center, the fortunes of William Brown faded.

He was forced to sell the house, and after the passage of time and several mortgages, it became the property of John Hoskins Stone, who was governor of Maryland for three years beginning in 1794. The mansion's subsequent history is hazy until 1823, when it was bought by Anne Arundel County as an almshouse, which it remained until 1965. That long-sustained usage meant that the building was essentially arrested in time and escaped the "improvements" so typical of many another eighteenth-century mansion that passed from generation to generation and one owner after another. Within three years of the last poorhouse resident's departure, the county decided to restore and furnish it as a historic exhibition building reflecting its colonial first-floor usage by Brown as a ferry-house tavern.

The mansion stands as the centerpiece of Historic London Town and Gardens, the gardens commemorating one of the town's best-remembered citizens, the physician and botanist Dr. Richard Hill, a contemporary of Williamsburg's eccentric garden enthusiast John Custis. Like Custis, Hill corresponded with the celebrated London horticulturist Peter Collinson and sent him samples of medicinal plants gathered in Anne Arundel County. Unlike the Custis-Collinson letters, however, most of Hill's correspondence has yet to be found. In the meantime a garden featuring plants mentioned by him has been constructed as an educational tool for London Town's interpreters.

Although the nationally designated historic area is the primary focus of Luckenbach and his Lost Towns staff, their efforts extend around the core site to include outlying plantations as well as others reflective of life and activity throughout the history of Anne Arundel County. Among these sites was one discovered by accident in 1991 when a bulldozer scored the edge of a small hill and exposed artifacts that included a lump of burnt clay with fragments of tobacco pipe stems built into it.

It turned out that the seventeenth-century owner of that Providence settlement lot had been one Emanuel Drew, whose 1668 inventory listed "a payre of Brass Pype Moyldes"—the two-part molds used in shaping clay tobacco pipes.

Rarely does an archaeological project yield some object or fact that elevates it above the ho-hum and "more of the same." The seventeenth-century helmets from Martin's Hundred were a classic example of the exceptions that prove the rule; Luckenbach's discovery of Emanuel Drew's 1661–68 tobacco-pipe-making operations is another. The oldest tightly dated pipe-making site discovered in the world, it has fragments of kiln furniture, varieties of clays, and examples of the pipes themselves that make this discovery of monumental importance to archaeologists on both sides of the Atlantic. It also makes nonsense of many conclusions hitherto reached about the nationality or racial origins of contemporary pipe makers working in Virginia. Indeed, some of the variegated red-and-white clay pipe fragments puzzled over in this writer's recently published *The Archaeology of Martin's Hundred* have their parallels amid the scores of fragments found on Emanuel Drew's Providence site.

In archaeology we must expect, indeed hope, to live and learn—which is what hundreds of schoolchildren do in their class visits to London Town to view the fruits of the Lost Towns Project. Each Wednesday afternoon throughout the academic year groups of as many as sixty students arrive to help screen the dirt being excavated by the professional archaeologists. Finding small chips of pottery, the occasional pin, buckle, or button, brings these young hands in direct contact with the past. For many it is an experience they expect to treasure throughout their lives—making them enduring supporters of London Town and the Lost Towns Project.

The road from Williamsburg, in the lower left of this section of a 1751 map, to Philadelphia, at upper right, led through London Town, labeled "London," southwest of Annapolis.

The reconstructed heart of the Fortress of Louisbourg: its chapel, governor's apartments, and garrison barracks.

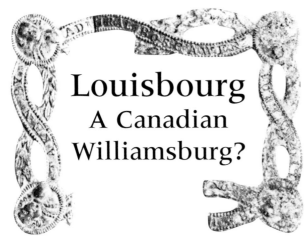

Louisbourg
A Canadian Williamsburg?

The portraits were tiny, four of them no bigger than a small toenail—a comparison suggested by their positions on the corners of a colonial-era shoe buckle (above). We found it in excavations behind the house of Williamsburg silversmith James Geddy II. Putting pictures on a buckle where only dogs would be likely to see them may seem a strange practice, but in the late seventeenth and eighteenth centuries brass founders, silversmiths,

and pewterers knew that there was a ready market for souvenirs of big events. Sleeve buttons were made for sale to patriots commemorating such occasions as the accession of Charles II, his marriage to Catherine of Braganza, and the coronation of Queen Anne. Indeed, wearing such buttons may have given rise to the expression "wearing one's heart on one's sleeve." But wearing it on one's shoes?

The Geddy buckle commemorated a victory of great American significance, namely British success in the conflict known here as the French and Indian War and in Europe as the Seven Years War. Additional evidence that Williamsburg citizens were concerned about the outcome of that conflict was provided by discoveries we made behind Wetherburn's Tavern.

Fragments of salt-glazed stoneware plates found there bear portraits of Britain's ally Frederick of Prussia and are inscribed, "SUCCESS TO THE KING OF PRUSSIA AND HIS FORCES." The shoe buckle, however, was more specific, for along with the four portraits came more information than any archaeologist had a right to expect. In raised letters it read, "LOUISBOURG TAKEN BY ADMIRAL BOSCOWAN JULY 26TH 1758."

The French settled in Nova Scotia in 1604 and called it Arcadia, meaning "the ideal region of rural felicity." This was something of an overstatement for a place ice- and snowbound in winter and frequently enveloped in fog or swept by winds capable of tossing one off into the sea. Nevertheless, it was the first landfall for immigrants to Canada, and anywhere that appeared solid under foot must have been considered more or less felicitous. Desirable or not, the British took it from the French at the end of Queen Anne's War and left them with two islands at the mouth of the St. Lawrence—Ile St. Jean and the much larger Ile Royale. The latter is today known as Cape Breton Island, and it was there, in 1713, that the French began building a fortress of seemingly impregnable strength.

Nestling in an oval-shaped bay, Louisbourg's harbor provided safe anchorage for fishing fleets as well as for warships capable of posing a threat to every coastal town from Maine to Georgia. With Anglo-French relations persistently strained, if not broken, the Louisbourg menace replaced the Spanish bogeyman of the previous century. Strategically, Louisbourg controlled the entry to the St. Lawrence

River and thereby the gateway to French Canada. Its ships also had the ability to disrupt cod fishing on the Grand Banks, a major facet of the New England economy. All in all, in the minds of the British, in London and in the colonies, a French military presence so felicitously located was not a good thing.

Had the French base on the Ile Royale been the only threat to the British-American colonies, a fleet out of Boston could have effectively blockaded it—as, indeed, the Compte de Grasse would do at the mouth of the Chesapeake Bay and York River in 1781. The French, however, were everywhere the British were not. Advancing from the south up the Mississippi in 1686, they put down roots at its confluence with the Arkansas River. They were at Mobile in 1702 and New Orleans sixteen years later. In 1720 they built Fort Charles and advanced further north in 1731 to establish a base they called Vincennes. And that was not all.

From Quebec and Montreal the French expanded southward to Fort Niagara in 1679, Detroit in 1701, Fort

Passez, mes amis! *Guards greet visitors arriving at the Dauphin Gate.*

Miami around 1704, and Fort St. Joseph in 1712, thereby controlling the Great Lakes and most of the lucrative fur trade. At the same time their Jesuit priests did their best to tame the Native American Iroquois toward Christianity and away from alliance with the British. Nobody enjoys having an enemy at his back, and that was precisely what the French pincer deployment had achieved. By circa 1740 every strategic internal location from the mouth of the St. Lawrence to the Gulf of Mexico was under French control. Meanwhile, the British colonies had expanded hardly at all.

Although the British were convinced to the contrary, there is evidence that the French advances were not a step toward sweeping them into the ocean, but only part of a benign plan to establish agricultural communities that stretched from the Lakes to the Gulf. For both sides, however, winning the Native Americans was seen as the key to success. Thus began the undeclared War of Brandy and Rum to win the Indians' favor and support. This, however, was one that brought the British some success, American distilled rum being available much more easily and in far greater quantities than French brandy.

From the outset, Louisbourg was as much a fishing harbor as it was a military base. Although the fortifications were begun in 1719, they were not completed until 1740. In the interim the stationed troops were employed as a construction force, while the harbor served as a maritime hub for French trade between Quebec, Arcadia, the West Indies, and France. Just as today, construction was likely to be more praise-garnering than maintenance. Consequently, the French engineers allowed what was already up to slowly fall down.

Supplies from France arrived slowly—if they arrived at all; the civil administrators

As in Williamsburg, the citizens of Louisbourg go about their eighteenth-century business not entirely oblivious of their oddly dressed, wrong-century visitors.

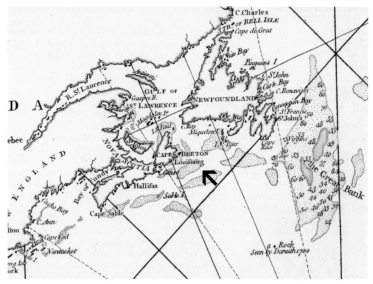

From their base in Louisbourg harbor, French warships kept vigil over the sea-lanes to Quebec. But it fell to the military garrison to repel the first British landing in Kennington Cove. Where children today build sand castles, General Wolfe's Redcoats were cut down in the water by heavy fire from the cliff top.

squabbled among themselves; favoritism and graft were endemic, as were drunkenness and gaming among the idle troops. Then came the War of Austrian Succession from 1739 to 1748, and once again treaty obligations set Britain and France at each other's throats. The British-American colonies, however, might have remained at ringside had not the French governor at Louisbourg received orders from Paris to do something useful. Consequently, he sent a small fleet commanded by Captain Du Vivier to attack and overrun the British fishing settlement at Casco in Nova Scotia. With that accomplished at minimal cost, Du Vivier was ordered to attack a less timorous target. He was to lay siege to Nova Scotia's capital at Annapolis Royale. In return, he so galvanized the jittery assemblies of the New England colonies that they sent a volunteer army of farmers and fishermen to take Louisbourg. And so they did.

During the following winter the New England volunteer garrison lost twelve hundred men to cold and disease, a far greater number than had been killed or wounded in the attack. Adding insult to injury, Britain's Aix-la-Chapelle treaty with France at the end of the war gave Louisbourg back to the French. Ten years later it would have to be attacked all over again, but this time by thirteen thousand British regular troops under Major General Jeffrey Amherst, and fourteen thousand sailors aboard sixteen transports and an escorting fleet of twenty-three men-of-war. The largest, the *Namur,*

Veteran Louisbourg archaeologist Bruce Fry, left, shows the author and his wife, Carol, some of the French faience found during the excavations.

with ninety guns and a crew of 780, was the flagship of Admiral Boscowan of shoe-buckle fame.

Although the expeditionary force was far more formidable than before, victory was less easily come by. The disaster in 1745 had taught the French defenders valuable lessons, and so they were ready for a landing south of Louisbourg. Those of us who have visited the scene of the American D-Day landings on Utah and Omaha beaches cannot help being struck by the similarity of events at the Cape Breton beach now called Kennington Cove. The day before the landing, a scout in a small boat had been sent to reconnoiter along the shore and did so without opposition. The surf, he said, was manageable and the coast deserted. But it wasn't. Hidden under brushwood, several hundred well-dug-in French regulars were waiting atop the fifteen-foot bluff.

Before dawn the morning of June 8, 1758, covered by the guns of the parent ships lying off shore, Brigadier General James Wolfe attempted to land his companies of grenadiers, Highlanders, and light infantry. No sooner had the first boats entered the surf than the French opened fire with muskets and grapeshot, slaughtering the defenseless grenadiers as they struggled in the water. Fourteen minutes later, it was over. Bodies, equipment, oars, and breached boats washed ashore to lie where today vacationers paddle and children build their sand castles.

Fortunately for the British, what could have been a debacle at Kennington Cove was salvaged when officers aboard retreating boats found another smaller cove immediately to the east and by outflanking the French, forced them to retreat. Penned in behind their once-imposing defenses the French prepared to withstand the siege, but the governor of the Ile Royale was not optimistic. All the French planning had been designed to stop the British before they hit the beaches. When that failed, he could only sit tight and hope that relief would come from France. De Drucour put it this way:

> This unfortunate occurrence which we had hoped to overcome [the landing], casts dismay and sorrow over all our spirits, with every reason, for it decides the loss of the colony; the fortifications are bad, the walls are in ruins and fall down of themselves, the outer defenses consist only in a single covered way which, like the main works, is open and enfiladed throughout its length; everything predicts a speedy surrender.

The British politician Enoch Powell has written that "the inevitable always takes longer than one expects." At Louisbourg four weeks passed without

Conservators like Jim Campbell maintain and study the extensive collections.

49

a British breakthrough. Six ships, three of them frigates, had been scuttled to block the harbor entrance, and behind them rode a small but not inconsequential fleet of French naval vessels. The six ships of the line and the remaining two of five frigates were sufficient to prevent Admiral Boscowan's men-of-war from sailing into cannon range of the town. On the debit side, however, had been the hurried departure of sixty Indians upon whom the French were relying. They had decamped on the first day of the attack, leaving with their equipment and supplies along with their spiritual advisor, the Abbé Maillard, who had decided that neither stoicism nor valor was his métier.

On July 21, a lucky shot ignited cartridges stored in the poop of the French warship *Célèbre*, sparks that set fire to the rigging and sails of other ships moored nearby. By dawn the next day, de Drucour's shipboard harbor defenses were no more. Six days later, the governor capitulated—to the relief of the civilian townspeople but to the fury of some of the French troops, who, to emphasize their disgust, broke their muskets and burned their colors.

Although such glory as was justified really belonged to Brigadier Wolfe and Major General Amherst, it was Admiral Boscowan as senior officer who accepted the surrender and who enjoyed the adoration of the crowds when he returned to England. This was the moment to sell souvenir shoe buckles.

In the following year the Ile Royale became the launching pad for the British advance on Quebec that would cost Wolfe his life. But that done, Prime Minister William Pitt was adamant that Louisbourg would never again pose a threat to the security of Britain's American colonies.

In the King's name he instructed Amherst in terms that brooked neither delay nor misunderstanding:

> It is His Majesty's Pleasure, that you do as expeditiously as the Season will permit, take the most timely and careful Care, that all the Fortifications of the Town of Louisburg, together with all the Works, and Defences what-ever, belonging either to the said Place, or to the Port, and Harbour, be forthwith totally demolished, and razed, and all the materials so thoroughly destroyed, as that no use may, hereafter, be ever made of the same.

To that end, some able engineers were sent out from England under the command of Captain the Honorable John Byron, grandfather of the poet. As contemporary historian Tobias Smollett put it: "By means of mines artfully disposed and well constructed, the fortifications were reduced to a heap of rubbish, the glacis was levelled, and the ditches were filled."

The fire-damaged barracks of the King's Bastion were to be repaired sufficiently to house a three-hundred-man British garrison, and privately owned houses were left intact—this on specific instructions from King George and his ministers. But because the French population of 3,540 people had been deported to France, the homes soon fell into ruin, spurred on by a fire in 1762 that threatened the town and was halted only after pulling down a dozen buildings in the flames' path.

When the last of the British garrison was withdrawn in 1768, most of the five hundred or so English and Irish families who had gone there after the siege departed along with the troops. The ruins of France's gateway to Canada were left to the fog, the ice, the seagulls, and the few hardy fisher families still scattered around the perimeter of Britain's new Cape Breton colony.

Two hundred years later the Canadian government embarked on an ambitious program of reconstruction, in part to provide work for laid-off Cape Breton coal miners, and in part to create a Colonial Williamsburg in the North. Work began in 1960, an event I well remember. I had been invited to apply for the job of archaeological director—which I declined to do. Several months later, however, because of a misunderstanding in the Canadian Park Service, I received a phone call congratulating me on having been selected. Declining so splendid an opportunity was not well received by the Ottawa official on the other end of the line. Nevertheless, my friend and Colonial Williamsburg colleague, archaeological conservator John Dunton, was more courageous or maybe more far-sighted than was I. He would work at Louisbourg until his retirement.

Today the King's Bastion, with its barracks, chapel, and governor's apartments, is again the centerpiece of the town that lies between it and the harbor. Military guards meet and, if we are friend rather than foe, greet us at the Dauphin Gate; once inside we are instantly transported to the 1740s to meet the people who lived and worked there. An aging Etienne Verrier, the engineer who designed much of the defenses, as well as his own palatial home, pauses from his plans to talk about his garden. Michel de Gannes, an officer of the *Compagnies franches de la marine,* had been there since 1722, and though a successful trader and land developer, he lives in a modest wooden home, having rented his larger stone-built house to his wealthy ship-sharing partner Antoine Rodregue.

What makes these people's homes and workplaces different from their Williamsburg counterparts is at first hard to define. But then it hits you. Nothing is old.

Unlike most historic houses, whose furnishings are antiques and whose curators lead us to believe that we are seeing them as they were way back when, the philosophy upon which reconstructed Louisbourg is based calls for everything to be new—as it was in 1744. Although only about a fourth of the site has been rebuilt, prolonged archaeological excavations unearthed precedents for countless artifacts, among them French earthenware from Rouen and Moustier, stoneware from Normandy, porcelain from China, along with glassware, tools, weapon parts, and the like. All have been reproduced with remarkable accuracy. When examples could not be found in the ground, paintings and engravings, as well as antiques in French collections, provided precedents for beds, chairs, chests, indeed almost everything contemporary inventories said should be in mid-eighteenth-century French homes and workshops. Thus, when we see a child's walker, it possesses none of the luster that only time imparts, nor, indeed, does it exhibit the superior styling that one would expect to see in a restored Williamsburg house. Instead, the cage-like device looks as though it was made yesterday—and maybe it was.

Louisbourg today may not be a Mecca for antique collectors, but, if we want to embark on an engrossing journey into the past, to do so we have only to satisfy the sentry at the Dauphin Gate.

In the mid-eighteenth century, ambitious and confident men had laid out their town on either side of a ninety-foot-wide avenue that pointed toward the mountains of Kentucky. It's still known as Stagecoach Road—Daniel Boone knew it well. Armies large and small passed this way: first the Regulators, ready to defy the might of Britain; then the enemy under Lord Cornwallis; less than a century later eager Confederate volunteers bound for battles too bloody to imagine; and later yet, General Sherman's pillagers returning north from Atlanta, the acrid smell of smoke still in their nostrils.

Thought by some to have been a slave quarter and kitchen, this stone-chimneyed structure is believed to be the oldest house still standing in a once-elegant but doomed town.

Williamsboro
An unlikely hiding place for the world's literary treasures, but . . .

Among the most hoary of conclusions is the adage that one thing leads to another. When I come to think about it—which isn't often—I remind myself that just about everything leads somewhere. Nevertheless, there are times when the linkage is so outlandish, so unexpected, that this particular cliché becomes a truism.

The story began in the summer of 1938, when amateur cryptologist Marie Bauer came to Williamsburg believing that the key to the authorship of the plays attributed to William Shakespeare lay buried in a vault beneath Bruton Parish churchyard. They had been brought to Jamestown by Henry Blount—the son of Francis Bacon—who upon arrival changed his name to Nathaniel Bacon.

The tangled and improbable web of evidence need not concern us here. In any case, it was laid out in the pages of *Colonial Williamsburg* in autumn 1992. All that matters now is to know that a somewhat bemused parish vestry gave Mrs. Bauer permission to dig, which she did until stopped on the advice of Colonial Williamsburg architects. In a subsequently published tract, she claimed that she was within an ace of finding the vault when permission to excavate was revoked.

Across more than half a century, disciples of Marie Bauer (by then Mrs. Hall) continued to believe that the proof, not only of the plays' authorship but also of documents such as a draft of the Declaration of Independence, had been denied to a

Top, the old "Hope place," abandoned and fast crumbling into ruin, is a sad reminder of better days. Bottom, outside the closed and shuttered general store, historian Phillip Evans and the author, middle, listen to local expert Lewis Almond point out how Daniel Boone went thataway.

welcoming world through "resistence by the Rockefeller Foundation." That myth took on new life in 1987 when the Veritat Foundation was created to push once again for the vault to be uncovered and opened. Four years later, students of the Hall doctrine arrived in Williamsburg, and once again churchyard dirt began to fly, and once again the diggers were evicted.

To lay the Bacon ghost to rest, Colonial Williamsburg archaeologists undertook a dig of their own, and to no one's surprise—save that of the Veritat Foundation—what had previously been thought to have been the corner of a buried treasure box turned out to be an ordinary eighteenth-century coffin. Twenty-nine years before, I had written *Here Lies Virginia*, a book that contained an account of the 1938 Bauer digging—a book that was read by Mrs. Ethel L. Cordingley in Cobourg, Ontario. For reasons never explained to me, she had sought the services of a psychic in Vancouver, who provided her with a "life reading" in a session recorded on audiotape. That was in 1974. In 1985, two years before the Veritat Foundation generated new interest in the Bacon controversy, Mrs. Cordingley read my book and was prompted to send me the tape. Her accompanying letter ended with, "Hope you get something from this if it's only a laugh."

The tape was scratchy and sometimes indistinct, but one aspect was abundantly clear—much of its content had nothing whatever to do with the life of Mrs. Cordingley. This is what the unidentified psychic told her:

> . . . there are retainers . . . and they followed him over on foot . . . stand up that it may be seen. We see that there are

Tutankhamen, the king whose discovery nearly put a curse on Dr. Goodwin's vision of a restored Williamsburg.

When Tut Went Phut; or,
The Day Mr. Junior Changed His Mind

*Rich Tomb Opened in Valley of Kings! Boy King Tutankhamen
Discovered! Tut's Tomb Greatest Ever Found!*

Headlines like these poured from newsrooms and ticker tape machines around the world. The public was agog with vicarious excitement. Tut songs, Tut dances, and Tut jokes were the rage of 1923. Not to be left out, in sleepy post–World War I Williamsburg, the corrugated iron door of a Duke of Gloucester Street garage invited customers to "Toot-an-Cum-In." None who saw the sign could have imagined that archaeological digging in faraway Egypt could threaten to change the future of their town. But it very nearly did.

Ever since Napoleon included scholars in his invasion of Egypt in 1798 and his defeat by the British in the Battle of Alexandria in 1801, the story of archaeology in Egypt has been dominated by national rivalries. In the nineteenth century it was between the British and French—with the French winning virtually every round. In 1902, however, a charismatic American Egyptologist named James Breasted secured a $50,000 grant from John D. Rockefeller Sr. to excavate in the Middle East. Seven years earlier Breasted had been named the United States' first professor of Egyptology where he taught, at the University of Chicago. And he had a dream.

Breasted wanted to establish a great center for Egyptological study at his university, and in 1919 he told his seductive tale to John D. Rockefeller Jr., who during the next decade contributed more than $1 million to create and foster the university's fledgling Oriental Institute. In 1923, after a thirteen-year absence, the Reverend Dr. W. A. R. Goodwin returned to Williamsburg from his pastorate in Rochester, New York, and he, too, had a dream. He wanted to restore Williamsburg to its glory years as the capital of the Virginia colony, and the man to do it, or so he thought, was Henry Ford.

Goodwin had previously written to Mr. Junior—as John D. Rockefeller Jr. was known to his associates—and invited him to contribute to the restoration of the College of William and Mary. The reply came from his private secretary, declining the invitation, saying that "it was not best for Mr. Rockefeller to assist at this trying time." The time, however, was not too trying to prevent him from continuing to bankroll Breasted's Near Eastern projects at a level of $10,000 per annum, and a year later to increase it sixfold. In 1924 Mr. Junior would contribute $60,000 to enable Breasted to excavate in Palestine at the site of the ancient city of Megiddo. Rockefeller would later allow that his growing interest in archaeology was entirely due to the influence of James Breasted.

While the Egyptologist's dream was becoming a funded reality, Dr. Goodwin's vision remained pennilessly transparent. His appeals to Fords, both Henry and son Edsel, bore no fruit. Having been run into by a Ford car while in Rochester, it is possible that Goodwin was a mite too aggressive in his approach. After extolling the virtues of Williamsburg as the heartland of American history, he chose browbeating:

"Unfortunately you and your father are at present the chief contributors to the destruction of this city," wrote Goodwin. "Garages and gas tanks are

In 1922, when Tutankhamen's tomb was discovered, John D. Rockefeller Jr. was already an enthusiastic promoter of American Egyptology.

Rockefeller's, top left, archaeological interest was captured first by Egyptologist Dr. James Breasted and then by the Reverend Dr. W. A. R. Goodwin, whose experience as an amateur archaeologist had been gained in 1905 while digging under Williamsburg's Bruton Parish Church, bottom left. Goodwin's success as a promoter followed Rockefeller's 1926 decision not to build a museum in Cairo to replace the antiquated displays then to be seen there, above.

fast spoiling the whole appearance of the old streets and the old city, and most of the cars which stop at the garages and gas tanks are Ford cars!"

Breasted's approach was, as we say today, less in your face. Mr. Junior found him a "charming gentleman and a distinguished scholar, with the modesty of the truly great." Consequently, when Breasted made his most ambitious proposal, Rockefeller's coffer remained open.

The Cairo Museum of Antiquities had been built in 1902 to the design of French architect Dourgnon, replacing one founded in 1858 by the great French archaeologist Auguste Mariette and filled by his successor, Gaston Maspero. It was not surprising, therefore, that the museum's labels were in French. The building was also poorly arranged and damp, and its basement storerooms prone to Nile flooding. Consequently, Breasted invited Rockefeller to build a great new museum that would do justice to the newfound treasures of Tutankhamen and provide

better housing for all that had previously been collected. And again Mr. Junior agreed.

In 1924 he set philanthropic funds aside for that project, instructing Breasted to oversee the planning as well as to make the first approach to the Egyptian government. In October 1925 Breasted took his plans and a handsome brochure to Egypt along with a letter from Rockefeller to King Fuad expressing his abiding admiration for Egypt's ancient heritage and offering a helping hand containing $10 million. In those days that was an enormous sum and one capable of answering all Dr. Goodwin's prayers, with more to spare.

Alas, in Williamsburg no angels sang. Henry Ford's well-known opinion that history was bunk was echoed by his spokesman, who answered Goodwin saying that his employer was "unable to interest himself in the matter mentioned." In February 1925 Goodwin again turned to Rockefeller, inviting him to visit Williamsburg, adding that "you

Built to a French design in 1902, the Cairo Museum had changed little when the author first visited it sixty years later.

can bring your pocketbook, or leave it behind." Goodwin was not the subtlest of men. Mr. Junior graciously declined.

And so did King Fuad. The proposed $10 million donation to build a new Egyptian Museum was unacceptable in its present form, Breasted was told. The plan had called for the finished museum to be administered by an eight-member commission: two Egyptians, two from the United States (one of them Breasted), two British, and two French. And that was the problem. Since the British Howard Carter had discovered Tutankhamen and Breasted had found Mr. Junior, the French would lose their controlling interest in Egyptian archaeology.

Back went Breasted to New York with a string of revisions that said nothing about French pique. Rockefeller was not amused but agreed to try again. Before the revisions could be made, however, a reporter for the *New York Sun* got wind of the stalled deal and published tongue-in-cheek letters to the king. "How many million dollars does

it take, Fuad, to make you jump?" reporter Amos P. Pipp wanted to know. If Mr. Rockefeller "offers you money for a museum he means a museum and will not attempt to add on a couple of big wings for oil stations." Always a private man, Mr. Junior did not appreciate the *Sun*'s attention. Nevertheless, he authorized Breasted to return once again to Cairo—where he met with more prevarication and a new set of demands.

The proposal offered $5.4 million for construction and $4.8 million for subsequent operating costs. But John D. Rockefeller Jr.'s patience was exhausted. There would be no $10 million for the Cairo Museum, and the pseudonymous Amos P. Pipp provided its epitaph. "You see what you went and done!" he wrote. "King, you spilled the beans. What you need is a business manager." That was May 4, 1926. Six months later, Mr. Junior visited Williamsburg to attend the dedication of Phi Beta Kappa Memorial Hall and provided Goodwin with a not-to-be-missed opportunity.

Inadequate labels, poor lighting, and no climate control prompted one recent guidebook to conclude that "in terms of display, [the Cairo Museum] may be the worst great museum in the world."

And of course he didn't.

If Goodwin had read about the debacle in Egypt, there is no record that he mentioned it when he guided Rockefeller around the remnants of eighteenth-century Williamsburg. It is highly likely, nonetheless, that he mentioned the magic word *archaeology* as he described the excitement of restoring the Christopher Wren Building, the reconstruction of the Raleigh Tavern, and the acquisition of historic sites and buildings. Goodwin had done his own archaeology inside Bruton Parish Church before its 1905 renovation, and one of his favorite books was the Reverend Frank D. DeHass's 1884 *Buried Cities Recovered or Explorations in Bible Lands*. It is safe to assume, therefore, that, before he was through, Goodwin had rung Mr. Junior's archaeological bell.

The rest, as they say, is history.

On more than one occasion Rockefeller said he was prepared to spend up to $5 million on the preservation of Williamsburg, but not a dime more. "Five million dollars," he said, "is a very large sum of money." Indeed, in those days it undeniably was.

From where, we may wonder, did that five million figure come? Was it the $5.4 million that King Fuad had let slip through his fingers? Had Professor Breasted succeeded in getting Fuad's minister's signature on the revised proposal, would Mr. Junior have been willing to share his interests in the grandeur that was Egypt with a matching concern for the future of a run-down, half-forgotten town in Virginia? We shall never know.

We do know, however, that the first archaeologist hired to dig in Williamsburg was one Prentice Duell, an architectural draftsman who stopped by for several months while on his way to another job. He was headed to Egypt to draw tomb paintings on behalf of Breasted and his Oriental Institute, funded, of course, by John D. Rockefeller Jr. As for the long-criticized Cairo Museum, it is now a hundred years old, a legally defined antique, and according to a recent guidebook, "It may be the worst great museum in the world."

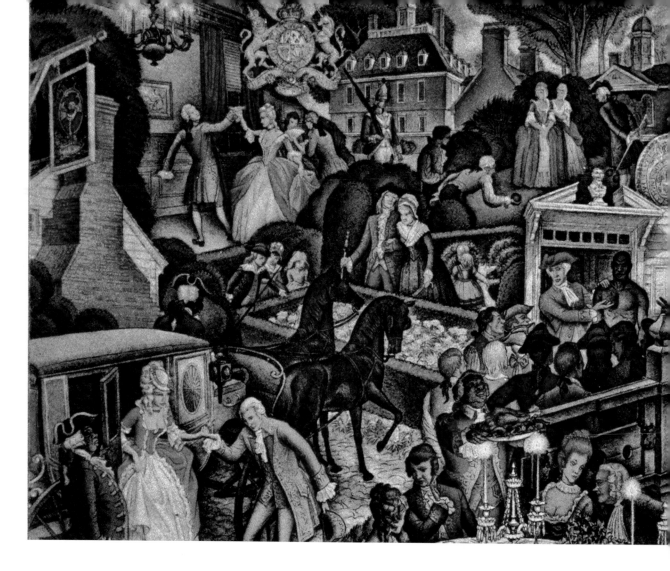

"Those Halcyon Days of Yore"
. . . when dreamers envisioned
working together "in one place"

With the opening of the Bruton Heights complex in 1997, Colonial Williamsburg entered a new age of educational excellence, and with it the capability to study, store, and conserve its wide-ranging collections in a research environment second to none. Seventy years having passed since the historic town began its transformation, the time was ripe for the Foundation to look toward the future and to its role in the twenty-first century. But, if we remember its motto, "That the Future May Learn from the Past," now is also a time for retrospection. And to that end I was invited to recall my impressions of Colonial Williamsburg as it was when I first came here as a short-term consultant forty years ago.

On a scorching August afternoon in 1956, Mario Campioli, Colonial Williamsburg's director of architecture, led me across the architectural drafting room past rows of tables behind which sat a phalanx of draftsmen, all deep in the pages of their evening newspapers. The papers were delivered around four o'clock, and it was understood that thereafter nobody did any work. It was too hot, and the Goodwin Building was not air-conditioned. Campioli pointed out the window in the direction of the parking lot behind Casey's store. "One of these days," he told me, "we're going to build a kind of Pentagon out there."

"A what?" I asked. I had only recently arrived from England and thought a pentagon was a five-sided anything. If I had heard of the Department of Defense's 1941 headquarters, I failed to make the connection.

"We'll have all our command units under one roof, the research library, the architectural office, archaeologists, the landscape architects, everybody working together, all in one place." A thin-faced and unsmiling man, Mario Campioli spoke wistfully about this prospect, as though it was a dream he doubted would come true in his lifetime. And he was right. It has taken another forty years for the dream to become a reality—and not in Casey's parking lot.

Alas, most of the dreamers are gone, their names remembered by only a handful of the Foundation's present staff: Sing Moorehead, Ernie Frank, Charlie Hackett, Bass Bridgeforth, Ed Kendrew, Paul Buchanan, John O'Neil, John Henderson, Jim Short,

This print, published by the West Virginia Pulp and Paper Company in 1938, reflects a romantic view of colonial Williamsburg markedly different from the revisionist, "warts-and-all" approach to the past that would gain popularity in the 1960s. In twenty-one events, symbols, and scenes, artist Ernest Hamlin Baker has brilliantly captured the spirit of eighteenth-century Williamsburg as the Reverend W. A. R. Goodwin and John D. Rockefeller Jr. may have envisioned it.

Campioli, young Mike Michelli, who left the drafting room to serve in Vietnam and gave his life for his country—the list goes on and on. No plaque is planned for the Bruton Heights School Education Center to honor those men for whom Colonial Williamsburg was both their love and their patriotic cause. But we who survive carry their faces in our memory, and, if the Reverend Dr. W.A.R. Goodwin was right in believing that the ghosts of Williamsburg's eighteenth-century patriots still walk its streets, we may be sure that the spirits of its architectural pioneers will haunt the new corridors.

Unlike most *National Geographic*–reading Americans, who at least knew of the beauty of the gardens, the graciousness of the hostesses in their ball gowns, and the thrill of seeing smoke belching from the maws of cannon as they saluted arriving tourists, I had not even heard of Williamsburg when Mario Campioli's invitation landed on my desk in London's Guildhall Museum. I arrived on July 3, 1956, to study glass in the archaeological collections.

Not only had I not heard of Williamsburg, but I knew nothing of the sweltering Virginia summer and so, on my first day's introduction to America, stood melting inside my English worsted suit as I watched the militia marching down Duke of Gloucester Street. The happy, flag-waving crowds were light-years away from my gray life and work amid the still bomb-blasted ruins of London.

Marching from the Capitol down the tree-lined roadway that President Roosevelt had called "the most historic avenue in all America," came the militia behind the scarlet-uniformed Fife and Drum Corps. Past the pristine white houses with their gleaming picket fences they came, past the shops of the peruke maker, the silversmith, and the apothecary, past the taverns and the stores marched the toy soldiers, and in their wake followed the neighborhood dogs and an assortment of small boys aping their elders, all mesmerized by the beating drums and the shrill notes of the fifes. For me, a foreigner—even one of the enemy—this was an experience never to be forgotten. It was, well, unreal.

I was not used to people, as I put it, dressing up in public—except, of course, for the Beefeaters at the Tower; and the infectious enthusiasm of the

Archaeological artifacts chosen for retention were generally those of architectural interest or that were well preserved. In the 1930s, wine bottles, like those being examined by conservator John Van Ness Dunton, top, were said to make up nearly 50 percent of the objects recovered. Everything deemed important needed to be marked with its site number—a task painstakingly performed by Sandy Morse, opposite top—then weighed and stored by type in metal boxes in the laboratory drawers, right. The rest were stored away in large wooden chests like those laid out, opposite bottom, in the auditorium of the Matthew Whaley Observation and Practice School during the excavation of the Governor's Palace in 1930. The archaeological collections were moved in 1957 to improved quarters, where they still remain.

Norman Rockwell–style crowd was new and fresh and wonderful. Those, we have to remember, were the Eisenhower years. World War II was won, the Nazi bad guys were long gone, and so was Joe McCarthy, and the president would run for reelection. Nobody much cared about Britain's problems over Cyprus or Egypt. It was summer, and the living was, if not easy, wonderfully tolerable.

In the previous summer, Colonial Williamsburg had turned itself into Hollywood East, and townspeople from vice presidents to Eastern State Hospital patients had slipped excitedly into knee breeches and ball gowns to play parts in George Seaton's yet-to-be-screened *Williamsburg—The Story of a Patriot.*

Across the railroad tracks beyond the Palace a great new complex was rising, the new Information Center Area—known to everyone as NICA—and in it not one but two theaters built to revolutionary specs especially to house the film and its equally revolutionary projection system. Although few had seen the rough cuts, lines from the script had already become part of the Williamsburg language: *English goods were ever the best. There is grave danger, but so few are aware of it! Are we so pusillanimous . . . ?* and so on.

The very heart, even the soul, of the Williamsburg experience was imbedded in the footage—duty, loyalty, right conquering over redcoats, contented slaves, and above all the sense of growing up in a new country rich in promise and filled with hope. It was unquestionably a movie of and for its time, and old folks who have seen it a hundred times still leave it teary eyed, yearning perhaps for their own lost youth rather than for a paint-and-powder world that never was.

The *Story of a Patriot'*s imagery of a Williamsburg awash with excitement and momentous activity and peopled by hat-doffing gentlemen and ball-gowned ladies had been captured much earlier in a long-forgotten painting by W.P.A. period artist Ernest Hamlin Baker. Although it has only recently reappeared—the cover of a surviving 1938 Westvaco paper mill publication—it recaptures far better than can any words of mine the romance of Williamsburg that was all around me on that Fourth of July in 1956.

Clutching my 1955 guidebook, I read that "each

visitor to Williamsburg today steps back across the bridge of years to the little city which for nearly a century was capital of the Virginia Colony and focus of a proud plantation society. Eighteenth-century buildings, furnishings, and gardens," the book went on, "again take their original form in this significant community." The gardens were, indeed, a joy to behold. Even though it was midsummer and the sun scorching, a small army of gardeners assaulted every weed and relentlessly trimmed any boxwood shoot that dared to mar the symmetry of its parent. Wherever one looked, there was order. Behind the Custis-Maupin house the parterre was inspired, so I was told, by the design of the British flag. Walking its brick and marl paths, I would never have guessed at its origin; but it was nice to think that eighteenth-century Virginians were that patriotic.

Whereas the symmetry of the Custis-Maupin garden was achieved in triangles, the Bryan House's garden proclaimed its sense of order through squares within squares. Resident landscape architect Alden Hopkins loved those gardens as might a mother; and a few years later, when a hurricane swept over Williamsburg, Hopkins, a kind and gentle man, was so appalled by the damage to his trees that he had a heart attack and died in his office.

Hopkins's predecessor, Arthur A. Shurcliff, had been certain that those who laid out individual Williamsburg gardens had subscribed to specific rules set down by the premier garden designers of their time. "The only dependable way to rediscover the old rules," wrote Shurcliff, "is to measure the ancient Virginia places themselves. Then the measurements should be drawn to scale and studied painstakingly with the contours of the ground, the vistas, the climate, the vegetation, the state of society and culture, and the documents of the time—painstaking," he went on, "because the Virginians took infinite pains with their places, gardens, and houses, and these do not give up their secrets quickly to him who runs, but rather to the one who is willing to devote time and labor to their study."

There was no doubt about it, the ruler and compass were evident wherever one looked, from the beds and topiary in the gardens to the sentinel shrubs on duty both at the corners of most houses and flanking their entrances. Small wonder was it that Williamsburg's restored gardens ranked high among the great gardens of the world. The interiors of the exhibition buildings reflected the same bandbox neatness that lesser mortals found so hard to maintain before the *House Beautiful* photographers came knocking at our doors. The furniture and furnishings reflected the dictum that English goods were ever the best, and for curator John Graham, when in doubt, buying the best of the best was best.

Writing in 1953, *Antiques Magazine* editors Alice Winchester and Edith Gaines, both longtime lovers of Williamsburg, saw these purchases as the product of "endless patience as well as the discrimination of true connoisseurship." They admitted that when it came to furniture, "archaeological evidence was not much help," but added that this was not so of other furnishings:

> A crew of workmen would descend on a site and start digging cross trenches 18 to 24 inches deep, removing a foot or two of soil at a time so that it could be carefully sifted. A ton or more of artifacts might be accumulated from one excavation—bits of clay pipes, broken wine bottles, fragments of porcelain and earthenware, rusted bits of ironwork. When this enormous mass of fragments was sorted and catalogued, sound archaeological evidence was available as to what had been used and in what ratio.

Curator Graham was less charitable. He advised at least one of his assistants not to waste his time with any of that junk.

Along with my invitation to visit Colonial Williamsburg on a three-month consultancy had come helpful copies of Goodwin's 1937 *National Geographic* article as well as more recent publications designed to give me a prior understanding of the place and its archaeological standing and facilities. Coming as I had from an archaeological laboratory housed in an attic of a partially bombed section of London's Guildhall, where the cold water pipes—we had no hot—froze in winter, and where benches and other equipment were cobbled together from other people's discards, the prospect of working in a modern laboratory was a lure too sweet to decline.

The lab would prove to be the antithesis of my London workplace, but not for the reasons I had expected. Where the latter was ice-cold, the Williamsburg lab was swelteringly hot, its humid hot air stirred but never cooled by a couple of overworked fans. Located in the maintenance and warehouse area, the lab was clean but simple, its only equipment an old domestic oven. The massed collections that I had read about were nowhere to be seen.

Neatly stored away in metal boxes on closed shelves and shut drawers was a small selection culled from the whole, each box labeled with its site designation and the collective weight of the shards housed in it. I was to learn that when one did not know what to do with anything, one weighed it—so many ounces of creamware, so many pounds of earthenware or porcelain selected from each site as being big enough or interesting enough to be kept. The rest, conservator John Van Ness Dunton explained, went over to the garage—or to an abandoned airport outside the town—to be stored unwashed in fish boxes. I later learned that an edict had come down from the architect's office that too many artifacts were being kept, and that henceforth no more than three filled fish boxes should be retained from any site. The overplus—as they would have called it in the eighteenth century—was thrown back into the refilled trenches whence it came.

Even at this controlled rate of ingress, the collections were growing at such a pace that something needed to be done. After I had been aboard for a few weeks, the head of archaeology and architectural research, Orin Bullock, asked me whether I thought anybody would be upset if word got out that the overplus had been dumped into the York River or into the closer-to-hand Lake Matoaka? He added, half in jest, that it might best be done at night. I told him that, night or day, either solution might be perceived as akin to Nazi book burnings. Needless to say, this was an idea that went no further—although after several weeks amid the grime of the fish boxes, I came to the conclusion that the modern champagne bottles and bits of farm machinery that made up much of the collection having no

The crash of demolition and the rough-and-ready methods of archaeological excavation employed in the 1930s made later practitioners shudder. But had modern, snail's-pace methods been used then, restored Williamsburg might well have been limited to isolated blocks around the Capitol and the Palace.

recorded archaeological provenance therefore had no probative value.

In addition to John Dunton, whose methods of preserving iron have stood the test of time better than much that has since been found, the conservation staff comprised a lone black man, Sandy Morse, whose job was to put numbers on the objects destined for the weighed and boxed "Study Collection." An old and careful man, Sandy epitomized the antebellum trusted servant who knew much, said little, but could be relied on to keep on doing whatever was asked of him—as long as it didn't involve hurrying. He was looking forward to retirement and the time when he could sit and watch the corn grow. One day when senior vice president Ed Kendrew visited the lab, he found Sandy slowly and deliberately painting numbers onto broken bottle glass. "Ah, Sandy," said he, "and how are you today?"

"I'm just fine, sah," he replied in that melodious southern voice that so reminded me of childhood years spent listening to the dialects of West Country farmers. Sandy did not look up.

"And what are you doing there?" Kendrew inquired.

If Sandy thought it a singularly stupid question, he didn't show it. He just went on painting his numbers. "Well, Mr. Kendrew, sah," he replied with the same deliberation that he applied to his numbering, "I'm just bidin' my time, just bidin' my time."

For me, that exchange seemed to capture the spirit of summer in Virginia and of a way of doing things that belonged to an almost forgotten era in Williamsburg, one both of steady accomplishment and of serenity. Twenty or so years later, an elderly lady who had lived here all her life put it best. She described it to me as "those halcyon days of yore."

Of course, that had not always been so. The first days and years of Williamsburg's restoration had been ones of frenetic activity, five or six excavations in progress at a time, new buildings coming down and old ones going up, a railroad shifted, churches rebuilt, schools torn down and replaced, all in the space of five tumultuous years that abruptly ended in 1933, when the ripples from the Wall Street crash finally came ashore in Williamsburg. The work of restoration resumed in 1936, albeit at a much slower pace, but came to a halt again in 1942 and was slow to gather speed after the war ended.

When I arrived eleven years later, the slow pace, so markedly different from the hubbub of ant-like Londoners streaming back and forth to work, became my abiding image of Williamsburg in the fifties.

Every major postwar decision continued to be dependent on: "What will Mr. Rockefeller think about it?" I was too junior ever to meet him, but his aura was everywhere and continued for years after his death in 1960. In the summer of 1956, the ancien régime was still in the Colonial Williamsburg saddle. Although the late Dr. Goodwin's vision had extended beyond building restoration and reconstruction to costumed interpreters meeting visitors at the railroad station, John D. Rockefeller Jr.'s project focused on the architecture. Consequently, from its inception the architects began and stayed at the apex of the administrative pyramid. Their goals were the driving force. Everyone knew where they were heading, and everyone shared the satisfaction of each project's completion.

It was almost like a family business, and for me that was strange but wonderful. I had come from a very socially structured society, where most people's place was ordained at the moment of birth—a place from which very few would escape. But here in Williamsburg, nobody thought it out of line for the senior vice president to go fishing or duck hunting with a warehouseman or the paint-shop supervisor. Although rarely if ever abused, that after-work camaraderie was both the glue that held the cart together and the grease that oiled its wheels.

And then there was the pride—the pride of the paint specialist excitedly peeling away layers on a window frame to reach the eighteenth-century color they called Apollo Room Blue, the pride of the carpenter creating a Chippendale bench for the Palace garden, and of the bricklayer carefully scoring the mortar between bricks, so confident that Mr. Rockefeller would approve.

There was, of course, a dark side, really more avoided than hidden. The confrontation at Little Rock was still in the future. The fact that the eighteenth-century population of Williamsburg had been half slave and half white was overlooked. My guidebook told me only that "the brutal slave trade still flourished" and then hurried to add that "besides the slaves, there were many white indentured servants." The book's editors saw no reason to list either slaves or blacks in their index. Although the Ku Klux Klan's flagpole erected in the 1920s at College Corner had been removed, the bench donated by Klan members was still there and would remain for several more years. As a registered alien from a country that had kept its racial problems overseas, I recognized the omission from Williamsburg's eighteenth-century interpretation, but I'm ashamed to say that I had no opinion about it. There was too much else to see and learn.

The Restoration's staff—as opposed to that of the hotels', of which I learned nothing—was by today's standards almost ludicrously small. Three people ran the personnel department, four were in the research department, and three more "ladies with green eye shields" were reputed to run the payroll and cash flow from an attic room on the third floor of the Goodwin Building. Out of its basement operated the audiovisual department under its inspired director, Arthur Smith, and his super secretary Kathy Yates, whose crew turned out prize-winning films that carried the Colonial Williamsburg story into classrooms from coast to coast and, through the State Department, into embassy libraries around the world.

In the space of three months I had met most of these dedicated people. My wife, Audrey, and I had cautiously sipped the coldest, most seductive martinis known to man in historian Howard Dearstyne's garden behind the Elkanah Deane House; we had been introduced to bourbon—I thought it had something to do with French kings—in Orin Bullock's basement under Marot's Ordinary, where amateur thespians met on Thursday nights to read plays. I well remember the bourbon—but not the third act of any play. I remember, too, how Campioli had taken us to meet Molly McCrea, the legendary mistress of Carter's Grove, and how architectural librarian Annie Parish had introduced us to the jungle-wrapped ruins of Rosewell.

Before we knew it, the three months were gone, and it was time for us to leave these kind and generous people who had made us so warmly welcome, time to leave the village that called itself the city where time stood still. We did so with leaden hearts, never expecting to see them or it again. Pausing in New York on the way home to the yellow fog of London in winter, we stood in Times Square on the night of October 31 and watched news written in lights atop the Times Tower. BRITAIN AND FRANCE GO TO WAR WITH EGYPT OVER SUEZ.

"Oh, no!" we sighed in unison.

A man standing in the crowd beside us muttered, "Suez, where the hell's that?"

Williamsburg, the enchanted city, already seemed very far away.

A new approach to archaeological excavation was adopted in 1957, the first hole being dug opposite Bruton Parish Church at the site of Peter Scott's cabinetmaker's shop, which burned in 1776. Forty years later the shop has yet to be reconstructed, notes the author, kneeling in the pit.

Suppose there had been a television antenna on the roof of John Page's seventeenth-century home. What would he have seen on the evening news?

You're Watching the *Colonial* Broadcasting System

Today's newspapers, magazines, radio, and, above all, television ensure that we have the world at our fingertips. Every piece of bad news is available twenty-four hours a day. If we are not moved by the plight of flood victims in Bangladesh on NBC, we can always switch to CNN for an in-depth report on rebellious Kurds or a volcanic eruption in Java. No more are the world's leaders imbued with an aura that makes us imagine them to be larger than life. The camera, and a press unconstrained by the fetters of propriety and good taste, bring them all into our living rooms stripped of majesty and respect. For these reasons, perhaps more than any others, the thinking of modern Williamsburg residents is fundamentally different from the thinking of those who moved there from Jamestown in 1699.

For most second-generation Virginians, the place they lived was the center of their world, and their neighbors—white, black, and Indian—were its population. Two rivers, the James and York, and an ocean to the east were together as confining as the stoutest chains. For the elite, however, the rivers and the sea were highways to a real or imagined homeland, and their interest in the world beyond the sea was much broader. The movers and shakers of colonial Virginia were as dependent upon European commercial and political stability as any modern international trader.

We, the heirs to those early Williamsburg residents, would soon be nervous wrecks if we had to wait six months to know whether our mail arrived safely in London, or whether a Parliament-led coup had sent the English royal family into exile and turned the status quo on its ear. In the living memory of Williamsburg's first colonial families, they had belatedly heard that their homeland had been torn apart by civil war, and that their king had been executed by victors whose names were known to but few Virginians. Plague had killed thousands, and London had burned down. Two more Stuart kings had come and gone. England had been to war with the Dutch, and, although nobody really won or lost, the British throne was handed to a Dutchman. For Virginians, none of these events were worried over as they happened. Neither cheering London crowds nor rumbling death carts had any impact. When, eventually, news of those nation-rocking events reached the colony, it was far too late for the average family to worry about them. Indeed, why should they? Something else could have happened to negate or change whatever it was that they would have worried over—had they known about it when it happened.

Let us imagine that in 1699, while living on the edge of Williamsburg in the fine brick house his great-uncle had built in 1662, John Page and his wife, Elizabeth, have converted their Jacobean court cupboard into a cabinet tastefully concealing a television. What would a wig-wearing Dan Flather have been telling them about the world at large? The CBS—Colonial Broadcasting System—anchor may have had difficulty pronouncing the name Preobrazhenskoe, but in 1699 it was the treaty of that name that carved up the once formidable Swedish Empire among Denmark, Russia, Poland, and Saxony. Had John Page relied on trade with the Baltic countries for his prosperity, the Treaty of Preobrazhenskoe would have given him cause for concern; so, too, would the mutual defense pact that had just been signed between Denmark and Russia.

For Virginians and for the English everywhere who used the Julian calendar, the last year of the seventeenth century would not end until March 24, 1700. Thus, were Page doing business with more progressive European countries, he would have clumsily identified the first three months of the new year as 1699/1700. Another half century would elapse before England's Lord Chesterfield put an act through Parliament to do what Peter the Great had done in 1699. The Russian czar shifted his New Year from September 1 to January 1, and, by order of the Diet of Regensburg, the Protestant German states did the same.

In London, the question of the English succession had been much in the minds of parliamentary leaders since the death of William III's Stuart wife, Queen Mary, in 1694. With the Protestant Anne, the second daughter of Catholic James II, as a logical and acceptable successor to William III, the question "What next?" should she die without issue was being debated as the century came to its end. The decision would be made to prevent a Stuart-led return to Catholicism by naming the electress of Hanover, Sophia, the eldest daughter of James I, to succeed. As luck would have it, Queen Anne and Sophia of Hanover would die in 1714, leaving the crown to Sophia's son, who thus became the first of England's four German Georges.

But that was all in the future. In the 1689 Battle of the Boyne, William III quashed the exiled James II's attempt to plant his standard in Catholic Ireland. But as the seventeenth century ticked away its final hours, James, backed by the powerful "Sun King," Louis XIV of France, was still alive and scheming. Consequently, he was regarded as a continuing threat to Britain's political and religious status quo—

and with good reason. A year later, when James II died, Louis proclaimed James's eldest son the rightful heir to the English and Scottish thrones.

On May 1, 1699, one of five student orators at the new College of William and Mary praised the growth of the Middle Plantation settlement that was now to be called Williamsburg. "Here are great helps and advances made already toward the beginning of a town," he said, and identified "a church, an ordinary [where Governor Francis Nicholson lodged], several stores, two mills, a smith's shop, a grammar school, and above all the Colledge." Had France chosen to restore the Stuart dynasty by invading England, the prospect of Virginians being asked to make their town's new name Louisburg or Jamesburg might not have been well received.

For the most part, the colony's planters were more concerned with practicality than with nomenclatorial cosmetics, and, for those with crops and goods to trade abroad, the nightly television news broadcasts summarizing the day's deliberations of the English Parliament would be reason for growing anxiety. In 1696, the old Navigation Act of 1651, barring British exporters from sending or receiving any goods aboard ships of nations other than their own, was rewritten with special attention to the practices of the American colonies. Now, in 1699, a new Woollens Act forbade them to export wool, yarn, or wool cloth "to any place whatsoever." Thus it became an offense to ship wool home to the English market even if carried aboard an English ship flying English colors.

The 1651 act was designed to assure English shipowners that they would no longer lose business to Dutch carriers. The 1699 act, however, had nothing to do with ships but everything to do with the prosperity of English sheep farmers and woollens manufacturers. The Virginia and New England colonies were barely producing enough wool for their own needs, but the principle rankled. The ho-hum acceptance of the 1696 measure was limited largely to those it did not concern. But for those obtaining or exporting contraband, London's attention was unwelcome. The act gave customs officers sweeping powers to apprehend smugglers and ordered the setting up of ten colonial vice-admiralty courts to try offenders.

In the eyes of many, smuggling was just another way of doing profitable business. Piracy, on the other hand, was something else. When the skull and bones of the buccaneers' black flag appeared on the horizon, it was a safe bet that not only would buyers and sellers lose their goods but, more important, the British government would be denied a shipload's worth of customs duties. Therefore, 1699 was to be the year Parliament issued an Act for the Suppression of Piracy. It would do little, however, to solve the problem in American waters as long as governors in Boston, Edenton, and Charleston found it profitable to turn a blind eye to buccaneers using their ports. In Pennsylvania a frustrated customs officer complained that known pirates "walked the streets with their pockets full of gold and are the constant companion of the chief in the government."

In Virginia, however, Governor Nicholson was determined to compensate for the laxity of predecessors who had allowed pirate vessels to berth in the bays and inlets of the Eastern Shore. On April 27, 1699, he presided over a General Assembly that adopted an act requiring that persons accused of "all Treasons Pyracys Murthers or Capital Offences committed upon the high Seas or in any River, Haven, Creek or Bay where the Admiral hath Jurisdicon" should be tried and sentenced "within this his Majesties Colony and Dominion."

There had been occasions, as Nicholson well knew, when the cloud of piracy could have a silver lining, as was the case when a trio of rovers were caught at the mouth of the James River, their small boat loaded with three heavy chests all filled with gold and silver treasure. Reviewing the seizure in March 1692/93, the king and his council had ordered that a portion of the loot—to the value of £300—should "be employ'd towards the Erecting [of] a Colledg or free Schoole in Virginia," thereby numbering pirates Davis, Delawafer, and Hinton among the first donors to the College of William and Mary.

For John Page, sitting smoking his pipe in front of his television, news reports of piracy would be too familiar to hold his interest past the headlines. Of greater moment was Louis of France and his American intentions. The Spaniards, who had long been Virginia's all-purpose bogeymen, were relinquishing their "scare value" to the French, who, for almost a century, had been consolidating their hold on the part of modern Canada they called New France. Now, in 1699, CBS was reporting incursions from the south. Exploring brothers, Pierre and Jean Baptiste Lemoyne, had landed on an island at the entrance to Mobile Bay as a first step toward establishing French colonies in the Mississippi Delta. In March, French priests from the seminary of Quebec encamped in Cahokia territory in Illinois as the vanguard of a movement of settlers from Canada and Louisiana. Advancing south down the St. Lawrence River and north up the Mississippi, French incursions into the Indian-controlled wilderness had the potential to drive the outflanked English settlements into the sea.

The accession of Dutch William to the English throne in 1688 brought the baggage of a war between Holland and France. That war spilled over into North America, where the English colonies became embroiled in the on-and-off fighting with the French and their Indian allies that came to be known as King William's War. Although it ended

This glass bottle is typical of those made for taverns in England.

with the Treaty of Ryswick in 1697, it would break out again as Queen Anne's War in 1701 and would continue for thirteen years.

Fortunately for Virginia, the administration of which was independent from New England's, most of the fighting was confined to the north. So, too, was the straightjacket of Puritan extremism that led to the terrifying Salem witch trials of 1698. Page's nineteen-year-old wife, Elizabeth, could happily dismiss much of the day's news as none of her business. It was a pity, though, that Williamsburg's planners had not set ground aside to build a theater. At London's Drury Lane, dramatist Colley Cibber's reworking of Shakespeare's *Richard III* was getting good reviews; so were George Farquhar's comedy *Love in a Bottle* and William Congreve's more enduring *The Way of the World,* which opened at the Lincoln's Inn Fields Theatre in March 1699/1700.

For an educated man like Page, a daily or even a weekly Williamsburg newspaper would have been a valued cultural asset; but for that his heirs would have to wait another thirty-six years. Scotland, on the other hand, had to wait no longer. The first issue of the biweekly *Edinburgh Gazette* was peeled from the press in 1699, joining six newspapers available in London. But, by the time copies could reach Virginia, the news was three months stale. Fortunately, not all news had to be wet off the press to remain of interest, and, in addition to regular newspapers, there were privately published broadsides to promote pet projects or points of view of more lasting interest.

On March 23, 1698/99, "James Thwaites Appellant" fired his own broadside at "John Deye, Gent. and Frances his wife, Respondents," over a £2,000 mortgage. In December, the Lord Provost of Scotland printed a sheet "forbidding the employment of women-servants for retailing liquors, as a great snare to the youth, and occasion of lewdness and debauchery." Another, this one by a cautiously anonymous author, was available from "the booksellers of London and Westminster. . . . Concerning the Murther of Mrs. Sarah Stout," who had been found drowned and whose charged killer had been acquitted. Yet another 1699 broadside focused on a murder almost seventy years old. Nevertheless, it was a case still able to intrigue even the most jaded

colonial *Nightline* viewer:

In the 4th year of Charles I. Johan Norkott was murdered by her throat being cut. Felo de se [a suicide verdict] was brought in, but 30 days after, the body was exhumed, and the four persons accused were placed in its presence. At the trial the Ministers of the parish, and of the next parish, made oath that the corpse changed colour, sweated, and opened its eyes and bled. On this evidence three of the accused were convicted and two of them, the husband and the grandmother, executed.

On a more upbeat note, it was reassuring to be told that, in spite of the Great Plague thirty-five years earlier, the century ended with London's population up from the 450,000 of 1660 to 550,000 by 1700, making it the most populous city in Europe. English populations in America also had grown to a century's-end total estimated at 262,000. About 70,000 of them were in Virginia, 5,000 in the town of New York, and 12,000 in both Boston and Philadelphia. Not so good was the news that in 1699 Philadelphia lost 220 to yellow fever and 150 more died of it in Charleston.

"This just in," intones Dan Flather. "English navigator and occasional buccaneer William Dampier, who so successfully sailed the South Seas to map the northwest coast of Australia and the coasts of New Guinea, is reported wrecked off Ascension Island. Now this important message."

A dozen white pills play leapfrog across the screen as harmonizing female voices sing the infuriatingly familiar jingle:

Within this place
Lives Doctor Case.
Here's fourteen pills for thirteen pence
Enough in any man's own conscience.

"Dr. John Case's pills for the speedy cure of violent pains without loss of time or hindrance of business are at your service, and are now available at . . ."

The screen goes blank. Elizabeth Page cannot abide commercials.

Some of the wine bottles made for John Custis of Williamsburg circa 1730 and found in the filling of his well.

New Messages in Old Bottles
Saved from being thrown into the York River, glass fragments reveal clues to the past

*I went to see Mr. Povey's elegant house . . .
and [admired] above all, his pretty cellar
and ranging of his wine bottles.*
—John Evelyn's diary, July 1,1664

"Our speaker tonight first came to Williamsburg in 1956 to study wine bottles." A voice from the audience asks, "Full or empty?" Everyone laughs at the originality of this sally, save for the speaker, who cringes and wishes the questioner all sorts of ill. It is true, nonetheless, that this writer did come to Williamsburg to do just that.

Archaeological excavations that began in the city in 1928 had amassed an enormous quantity of broken bottles dating from the eighteenth and nineteenth centuries. With the exception of a few found either whole or in sufficiently large pieces to be put together, most of these treasures were housed in legions of wooden boxes stacked ceiling high in a warehouse. Throughout the first twenty-eight years of Williamsburg's reconstruction, excavated domestic artifacts contributed little to historical interpretation. They were merely stuff to be rounded up—if in large-enough pieces—to store until such time as someone who knew enough to recognize them came along to sort them out. That bottle fragments could be the key to dating the ground in which they were found never occurred to the early excavators.

After nearly three decades of digging, the accumulation of broken bottle glass had become a major storage problem, prompting Colonial Williamsburg architects—who at that time directed the archaeology—to consider seriously burying it or throwing the lot into the York River. One or the other of these draconian solutions had yet to be implemented when, in 1950, the National Park Service's senior archaeologist, Jean C. Harrington, went to London in search of anyone who might know something about Jamestown period glass. He found me.

Five years later Harrington was asked whether he knew of anyone in England who might come over to do something with Colonial Williamsburg's archaeological collections. Knowing that they included large quantities of broken bottles and remembering his encounter with a young student of bottles who was then the City of London's archaeologist at its Guildhall Museum, he was able to call my name to mind. The rest, as they say, is history.

As no precise records had been kept to show where the multitude of bottle fragments had been found, there was very little that could be said of them—beyond the obvious fact that Williamsburg property owners had used bottles of various types throughout the colonial eighteenth century and beyond. Although that conclusion was hardly worth the transatlantic ticket, the collection did demonstrate that while most of the shapes fitted readily into an evolutionary progression from squat to tall, a few were of types hitherto unrecorded, notably two varieties made for Duke of Gloucester Street storekeeper John Greenhow, one dated 1769 and the other 1770.

The earliest Virginia-related bottle of shaft-and-globe type was made for Ralph Wormeley of Jamestown and Rosegill, who died in 1651. It was found in London.

Of narrow-necked bottles—like narrow-souled people—Alexander Pope wrote, "The less they have in them the more noise they make in pouring out." Illustrating the point is the detail from William Hogarth's 1755 engraving Election Entertainment, *which shows several bottle shapes attributable to the 1720s and 1740s.*

My London research into the evolution of the glass wine bottle grew from a need to date the accumulation of soil and the man-made intrusions cut into it. From the first years of their creation in the late 1640s, bottles made for individuals and particularly for tavern and innkeepers were frequently identified by the application of glass seals—sometimes referred to as buttons—to their sides and shoulders. Perhaps 20 or 30 percent of such seals also bore the dates, either of the bottles' manufacture or of their contents. By studying the various forms identified by dated seals, a simple shape progression could be established, one that applied as well to bottles without seals as to those with them. Because bottles, second only to clay tobacco pipes, were the most frequently broken and discarded of colonial-era artifacts, the value of this type of series was incalculable. Thus, for example, the total absence of these post–circa 1645 bottles from the several early sites excavated at Martin's Hundred provided the strongest possible evidence for the abandonment of Wolstenholme Town and its environs before that date.

This is not to say that in early seventeenth-century Virginia nobody possessed wine or spirits in bottles. On the contrary, fragments of many were found on the Martin's Hundred sites; but they were all blown into square molds and, after being finished by hand, they resembled those made in Holland into the nineteenth century, primarily as containers for gin. The early square bottles were transported and housed in compartmented boxes called cellers or cases, but, once removed from the boxes' protection, their flat sides and sharp corners made them easily broken. That shortcoming gave rise to thick, green-glass, globular bottles with long necks popularly known as shaft-and-globe, which in their day were simply bottles for wine, ale, or anything that came as a liquid. Besides being stronger than the case bottles, the new shape had the advantage of being able to be binned upside down, so that the corks could be kept moist and tight.

The earliest dated specimen, surviving only as a seal, was found in the River Thames and is stamped W E 1650; but the first to display an identifiable name has a familiar American ring to it, that of John Jefferson and the date 1652. First recorded in 1949, that seal long remained the earliest dated example on record. However, it was not representative of the earliest tightly datable bottle to survive—albeit barely. In 1954, a friend happened to be passing a bombed building site in the city of London and heard the sound of laughter and breaking glass. Looking over the roadside barrier into the basement below, he saw a group of workmen throwing green-glass bottles against a wall. As missiles, they were undeniably tempting, for their long necks and heavy globular bases were reminiscent of German hand grenades. The workmen let my friend salvage some of the pieces; and, knowing my interest in bottles, he gave the fragments to me. From them, two bottles were restorable, each bearing an identical seal impressed with two initials: R.W.

Bottle buyers who wanted the best had brass dies made with which to stamp their shields of arms, crests, or tavern signs; but others, content with no more than personalized identification, settled for dies made up by the glassmaker from an alphabet of separate initials. Both R.W. seals displayed the same haphazard association of the dies, one set slightly higher than the other.

Typical sealed wine bottles from circa 1660–1823.

I never expected that it would be possible to identify R.W., for there could have been dozens of people with those initials living in mid-seventeenth-century London. It turned out, however, that the owner was not in London but in Virginia.

While studying Colonial Williamsburg's bottles, I also found time to review those found at Jamestown. There, to my astonishment, I came upon an identically arranged R.W. seal that had been discovered on a lot once owned by Ralph Wormeley of Rosegill. As he died in 1651, his London bottles can claim to be the earliest known datable examples, and their accidental discovery must rank among the

probably in Oxford, where a shorter necked bottle now in the Ashmolean Museum has a seal with an almost identical castle and the only partially legible name RICHARD [BI]LLINGSLY.

That bottles made for English inns and taverns should stray was by no means unusual. The only intact bottle so far found at Jamestown dates around 1655 and bears a seal displaying three feathers—probably a Prince of Wales tavern or inn—and the incomplete name ——PH FR——. As a long shot, this might be Joseph Franklin, who lived at Bridgewater in Somerset and issued a trade token in 1666. Another survives only as a seal impressed with the initials

scarcely believable coincidences in the short history of historical archaeology. One Wormeley bottle is now in the Corning Museum of Glass, and the other is back in England in the Museum of London.

Of only slightly later date is another found in recent excavations at the site of John Page's house that stood on the outskirts of Williamsburg in the area since occupied by the new Bruton Heights School Education Center. The bottle's undated seal depicts a rose over a castle, both under the name R. BILLINGSLY. No individual of that name is known to have been in the Virginia colony in the mid-seventeenth century, and it is highly likely that he was the landlord of a Rose and Castle tavern,

E H beside a bell, and yet another is inscribed H TVRNER AT THE [VINE] around a cluster of grapes.

Errant tavern bottles are not necessarily the product of thievery—as excavations on the site of Robert "King" Carter's burned mansion at Corotoman would seem to have proved. The fragment comes from a bottle of about 1720, its seal identifying it as the property of Thomas Great, landlord of the Two Twisted Posts tavern in Colchester. That the immensely wealthy Carter would have stooped to stealing Tom Great's bottle is an intriguing but unlikely possibility.

Another rover is a unique specimen of half-bottle size in my own collection that bears a rose on its seal and the initials W M H. A faded label on its base records that it was "Dug up in Mrs. Anstey Perks' garden, Breaston, Derbyshire." For more than thirty years I assumed that this circa 1665 bottle came from a Rose tavern in that county—until excavations in Nottingham yielded a bottle with the same seal from a site only two lots away from a Rose tavern.

As the seventeenth century progressed, the almost spherical-bodied bottles developed an angled shoulder and a gradual reduction in the length of their necks. Several examples found at Denbigh Plantation—once Mathews Manor in Virginia's Warwick County—represent the transi-

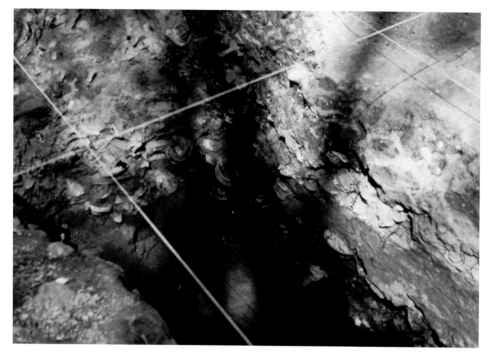

Excavation of an old cellar on Williamsburg's South England Street revealed a solid layer of broken bottles, left, from the second quarter of the eighteenth century. A group of typical wine bottles of the 1680s, opposite, was found during construction clearance at Denbigh Plantation in nearby Warwick County.

tion to a wide and squat form that collectors call "onion" bottles but that, to my eye, look not in the least like onions.

Although onion bottles are common from Williamsburg excavations, the earliest was unearthed from an unknown context adjacent to the Armistead House, whose site has been excavated by Williamsburg archaeologists. However, the bottle was not found by them but was discovered and bought by an antiquarian book dealer after he came upon it in the attic of the early twentieth-century frame house shortly before it was moved from Duke of Gloucester Street to a new location outside the Historic Area.

Some of the best examples of early eighteenth-century bottles were found in the well at the John Custis House (discussed in *Colonial Williamsburg,* Summer 1994), several of them marked I. Custis and others John Custis 1713, all of them now enjoying a treasured place in the Foundation's archaeological collections not only as early bottles but for their association with the father-in-law of Martha Washington. Other bottle-owning Williamsburg worthies included Governor Francis Nicholson, signer George Wythe, merchant Thomas Hornsby, whose seal is dated 1769, and his nephew Joseph Hornsby, his seal dated 1774, as well as two other Williamsburg merchants, John Blair, dated 1731, and an undated Samuel Cobbs.

Just as some seventeenth-century tavern bottles reached Virginia under questionable circumstances, so later did others made for Englishmen who—at least to our knowledge—never set foot in America. One such bottle bore the seal of the first Earl Powlett, who was nominated a Knight of the Garter in 1712 and who lived until 1743. How his broken bottle came to be found near Anthony Hay's cabinet shop on Williamsburg's Nicholson Street is anybody's guess.

Collectors usually call these all-purpose vessels *wine* bottles, but cautious curators often prefer to

describe them as beverage bottles—although one does not as a rule drink paint, fuel oil, or lead shot, all of which have been found in excavated bottles. That squat onion bottles were used as containers for wine, there is no doubt; nor is there any denying that they were used for bottled ale, full examples of which washed ashore in 1955 from a ship wrecked off England's Kentish coast in 1702.

Perhaps the most remarkable evidence of standard bottles of the 1740s being filled with a potable liquid other than wine or beer was discovered during the restoration of Wetherburn's Tavern on Duke of Gloucester Street. Excavating beside the building's foundations, we discovered a cache of fifteen carefully buried bottles, all containing black Morello cherries. Later, more groups of these buried bottles were found, ten of them beside the kitchen and yet more adjacent to the dairy. Most of them contained cherries, one of them with the remains of 249. To determine their bulk when fresh, we inserted that number into the same bottle and discovered that they left no room for liquid. We also found that once in we couldn't get them out! Consequently, we have never been sure whether Henry Wetherburn was making cherry brandy, brandied cherries, or simply bottling cherries. One conclusion was inescapable, however: His was the largest number of intact bottles ever found on a Williamsburg site.

Although once-empty seventeenth- and eighteenth-century English bottles rarely provide clues to their original content, now and again an owner would scratch that information into the glass with a diamond or even a common nail in a process known as pricking. One such bottle is inscribed WINE and

That narrow-necked bottles had a long life is confirmed by the narrow neck, opposite, "C," marked RS 1764. It ended up in Massachusetts. Of much earlier vintage are examples "A" and "B," the first a unique half-bottle size of circa 1660 that bears the seal of a Rose Tavern in Nottingham, England; the other, dating to about 1685, from the Armistead House site on Duke of Gloucester Street in Williamsburg. Farther up the street, merchant John Greenhow sold liquor in three bottle shapes, one of which, "D," is dated 1769. Mid-eighteenth-century bottles "E" and "F" were filled not with spirits but with mineral waters from spas at Pouhon in Belgium and Pyrmont in Germany. The Pouhon bottle is cased in sewn canvas and strapped with leather.

dates around 1730, while another made in the same decade is inscribed RS 1764—a reminder to archaeologists that some bottles continued in use long after they were made.

Bottle types akin to the English shapes but made in eighteenth-century Europe reached Virginia in relatively small quantities, and a few unmarked Dutch and French examples have been found in Williamsburg excavations. More readily identified, however, are bottles made to transport and store mineral waters, for these are usually marked with a glass seal as coming from spas in modern Belgium and Germany, specifically those of Pouhon and Pyrmont. The former are ovoid, look like a deflated balloon, and because of their fragility were encased in wicker or in an elaborate jacket of glued canvas and leather strapping. The Pyrmont bottles, on the other hand, were much stronger and needed no such protection. Both are reminders that many Virginians, King Carter among them, worried about their health and drank bottled spa waters as we do Evian and Perrier.

After a more artifact-oriented approach to archaeology became standard in Williamsburg, the vast quantity of dust-gathering bottle fragments in storage were rendered even less useful and informative. Once again the question of what to do with all that undocumented glass became an issue in need of a solution. Neither reburying it nor secretly tipping a truckload off the Yorktown bridge had much appeal. Instead, I came up with what I considered a Solomon-like answer. With the 1976 bicentennial approaching, why not, I suggested, melt it down and make it into new bottles adorned with seals commemorating the occasion? As rare souvenirs of the celebration, they could be sold at an immodest price that would cover the cost of production while providing a profit margin of mouth-watering dimensions.

As expected, this masterly solution appealed to marketing gurus and space hungry colleagues, and under my supervision large quantities of broken glass were trucked out to West Virginia to be hand-blown into new old bottles of a shape characteristic of the Revolutionary War era. The first hitch occurred when the glass factory management advised me that it could not make the bottles entirely from

Packaged for the bicentennial, this bottle was one of the few acceptable reproductions. The rest were consigned to the Palace cellars, where the author, below, ponders his boxed-bottle idea.

shape, the blowers and marverers—those who do the hand shaping—puffed and marvered mightily to come up with bottles whose bases were too thick or too thin, whose necks were too long or too short, and whose string-rims (the cordon of glass around the lips to hold wires or strings) were too high, too low, or of the wrong shape. Thus, out of the several hundred ordered (each to be handsomely boxed and given a limited edition number), only about 25 came within a country mile of being right. Thanks to my brilliant idea, we had exchanged our unwanted broken bottles for a massive supply of equally unwanted intact bottles.

They survive to this day, not as treasured bicentennial souvenirs in the cabinets of discerning collectors, but bottoms up, their shortcomings disguised by a bed of straw, in the wine bins of the dimly lit Governor's Palace cellars. Needless to say, I was not invited to come up with any further merchandising proposals.

the old glass. It would have to be mixed with new glass in an old-to-new ratio of no more than forty percent.

Unaccustomed to blowing bottles from such a mix and being unused to the required colonial

Although it is unlikely that a trial would have been conducted at night, the 1706 ordeal of Grace Sherwood, the Virginia Witch, is otherwise authentically reenacted at the reconstructed Capitol in one of many evening experiences available to Colonial Williamsburg guests. Goodwife Elizabeth Hill, portrayed by Lynn Evans, points the finger of accusation against Sherwood, portrayed by Diane Landon.

Witchcraft and Evil Spirits
"Weird sisters, hand in hand . . ."

*To use or practice Witchcraft, Inchantment, Charme,
or Sorcery, whereby any person shall be killed,
pinned, or lamed in any part of their body,
or to be counselling or aiding thereto, is felony.*
—The Countrey Justice

Such was the law in England when the first Jamestown colonists brought those same laws with them to Virginia. Today, to most of us who have never been on the wrong side of a gaolhouse door, a felony is vaguely recognized as a crime as trivial as shoplifting or as heinous as assassination, and that rarely does the felon pay with his or her life. In the eighteenth century, however,

death could be the penalty for "divers Particulars," and witchcraft was numbered among them.

Contrary to popular legend, in the sixteenth and seventeenth centuries witches condemned in England were hanged and not burned, as they had been in Scotland and throughout Europe in previous centuries. A felony being a crime below the level of *petit treason,* under English law those convicted of it were spared the stake, that being reserved for the highest crimes—like counterfeiting the king's coins. As late as 1794 diarist John Stedman noted that henceforth "no more women [were] to be burnt for coining as formerly, but to be hanged to the gallows as men. This certainly is an amendment," Stedman added.

But the prospect of hanging, or more often drowning, following a charge of witchcraft was enough to evoke terror in the mind of the accused. Indeed, it was not unusual for fear, coupled with physical persuasion, to draw the wildest confessions from the frail and the innocently foolish.

What is it about witchcraft, one wonders, that continues to fascinate the public and that has made Colonial Williamsburg's *Cry Witch!* one of its most popular dramatizations? Is it perhaps the lingering result of childhood fears of bogies beneath the bed or the creaking of a cupboard door in the darkness of the night? Or is it the suspicion that the Prince of Darkness may really exist and that some people might truly have sold their souls to him?

Skeptics like myself have only to respond to the Internet's invitation to enter the right keyword to discover that witches are alive and prospering and may even be counted among our own neighbors. Indeed, a recent fact-finding trip to the site of America's most notorious witch hunt, elicited the freely provided assurance that no fewer than 3,000 practicing witches and warlocks currently make their home in Salem, Massachusetts.

Virginia, however, hasn't tried a witch since 1706, but it may be no coincidence that it occurred in the lifetime of many who remembered the horrific outcome of the Salem trials of 1692. To put the Williamsburg ordeal of Grace Sherwood in the context of its time, we have to look—albeit briefly—at the events that led up to and generated the Massachusetts frenzy.

Clockwise, character interpreters Steve Holloway, Tom Morgan, Cathy Bortz Palmer, and Tom Hay take their parts in the tableau. Serving for the jury, the audience decides whether Grace is guilty of bewitching her accuser and causing her to miscarry. The final fate of the real Grace, who lived and was tried in what is now Virginia Beach, is no longer known.

The majority of the New England leadership had settled there in pursuit of religious freedom, at least for themselves. That freedom centered on the strict interpretation of Scripture and thereby rendered their spiritual leaders as close to God as they could get. But, as in England, the rural and urban populations of the Salem township were prospering from life in a mercantile and fishing port, while to the north the rural area of scattered farmsteads was less prosperous and in physical terms, more hard working—and increasingly resentful of the fact that Salem Village was administered both legally and spiritually by the town elders. It was to Salem Town, therefore, that the farmers had to go to attend civic gatherings, they having no meeting house of their own. Nor did they have their own church or their own minister.

As the years slipped by, the battles of words between village and town grew ever more heated, and even when, at last, in March 1673, the General Court permitted the villagers to build a meetinghouse and to hire their own minister, they were still dissatisfied. In Puritan doctrine a meetinghouse was not a church. That was a term set aside to define a select group of elders who made themselves the voice of the rest, who were lumped together as the congregation. In Salem Village, those living closest to the town associated themselves with it, while the distant farmers had little input beyond paying their taxes. In short, neighbor was pitted against neighbor, the men resentful and adamant in their beliefs and their womenfolk poisoning interfamily relationships with their gossip.

Into this volatile mix, like children playing with matches beside a powder keg, a group of village girls amused themselves creating a secret circle that rotated around Tituba, a West Indian slave brought from Barbados by the then-current minister, the Reverend Samuel Parris. Tituba was an exotic figure amid this grim-faced community and encouraged Parris's daughters (among several others) to dabble in fortune-telling and in magical experimenting. When the girls became so caught up in the game that they began to act irrationally, their parents grew suspicious, and, when the village doctor had no cure or explanation, fear and speculation spread beyond the Parris household. Meanwhile, other village girls and women began to go into lunatic convulsions. At first muted and soon increasingly clamorous, the cry of *Witch!* was heard throughout the village community.

Hogarth engraved a broom-riding witch feeding a black cat.

What happened thereafter was to become a well-known chapter in American history. By the time the frenzy abated eighteen people had been hanged, and more than a hundred condemned or alleged witches languished in Boston jails through the summer of 1692, among them a four-year-old girl who spent the best part of a year in chains. That these people escaped the hangman's noose was the product of a coincidence that was to make its mark in Virginia. In 1690, when news of the overthrow of Britain's Stuart monarchy reached the colonies, Sir Edmund Andros, then governor of the Dominion of New England and a future governor of Virginia (1692–98) was the victim of a coup d'état and found himself jailed in Boston.

Andros's successor, Sir William Phipps, did not arrive there until May 1692, and, although the witchcraft frenzy was then at its peak, he at first did nothing to halt it. Instead, he gave legitimacy to the witch hunters by appointing his lieutenant governor to head a commission to try the accused. By the autumn, however, Phipps had changed his mind and put an end to the trials—perhaps because by then his own wife had been named in the ever-growing register of the Devil's disciples. Those of the convicted who were still alive were pardoned, and those still awaiting their day in court were released, thus writing finis to the darkest page in the annals of colonial Massachusetts.

Against the backdrop of New England's Puritan hysteria, the case of Virginia's Grace Sherwood was no more than a minor aberration, remembered primarily because she was put to the long-established test of swimming. According to law, a suspected witch was to be bound hand and foot—or rather thumb and toe—then thrown into a river or pond. If she floated, she was guilty; if she sank, she wasn't. Although not an altogether satisfying repudiation for the innocent, Grace Sherwood "by her own Consent [agreed] to be tried in the water by Ducking."

Grace and her husband, John, were an impecunious farm family resident in Lynnhaven Parish in Virginia's Princess Anne County. In 1698 they had filed suit against two neighboring couples for slander. Defendants John and Jane Gisborne were alleged to have accused Grace of being "a witch and bewitched their pigg to death and bewitched their Cotton." Elizabeth Barnes claimed that Grace had come to her in the night "and rid her and went out of the key hole or crack of the door like a black Catt." In both cases the courts ruled in favor of the defendants. In the same year and in the same district, another couple, John and Ann Byrd, brought suit against Charles Kinsey and John Potts in country court, charging that they had been falsely accused of being witches and in league with the Devil. In each case the jury found for the defendants.

It is curious, indeed, that this outbreak of witch mania should erupt in a relatively poor farming community reminiscent in some measure of the backwoods nature of Salem Village. However, the history of witchcraft in colonial Virginia was not confined to that place or to that time. The first Jamestown colonists had left England awash with witchcraft. Its king, James I (and VI of Scotland), firmly believed that his Catholic rival, the Earl of Bothwell, had unsuccessfully used witchcraft in order to have him drowned at sea. In the frenzy of denunciation that followed, two hundred alleged members of Bothwell's coven were accused of having held a sabbath in the church at North Berwick, where he had appeared to them as the Devil himself. Three women among the accused were tortured in the king's Holyrood Palace and confessed that they had ridden to sea in sieves and by throwing dead cats into the water had caused the tempests to erupt. There can be little doubt that Shakespeare had the Berwick trials in mind when, in *Macbeth*, he had his first witch declare, "Her husband's to Aleppo gone, master o' the Tiger: But in a sieve I'll thither sail, and like a rat without a tail, I'll do, I'll do, and I'll do." Although Bothwell escaped into the Scottish Highlands, the three women charged as leaders of

The universal fascination with witchcraft is illustrated in this painting by Latvian artist Bernhard-Christian Borchert, reminding us that coven membership was open to impressionable youth as well as to the midnight hags of Shakespeare's imagination.

his witches as well as one man, who under torture confessed to being the Devil's secretary, were all burned at the stake in 1591.

Six years later, James published his witchcraft tract titled *Daemonologie,* and in it assured his readers that the Devil could manifest himself "in the likeness of a dog, a cat, an ape or such-like other beast" and that his followers were able to make their victims fall sick by mutilating wax images. In 1604, the first parliamentary year after James became king of both Scotland and England, a harsh statute called an "Act against conjuration, witchcraft and dealing with evil spirits" was adopted and remained in force in Britain and in her colonies for more than a century. Replacing earlier witch-related laws, the new one was the first in England to condemn a proven witch to death. Out of this code, in 1611, emerged the first edition of Michael Dalton's *The Countrey Justice*, which summarized the existing statutes for the benefit of local courts and justices of the peace.

At least one copy of Dalton's helpful volume was in the hands of Virginia jurists in 1675 when the book was cited in the charge against suspect Jane Jenkins, she "being familiar with evill spiritts and useing witchcraft." The discovery procedure was then stated to be performed "according to the 118 chapter of doulton." That trial took place in Lower Norfolk County, the district whose name was soon to be changed to Princess Anne—and home to the about-to-be-ducked Grace Sherwood. Although we know of several such charges (most of them dismissed) in that region, one has to remember that few such records have survived for other counties—counties which may well have had as many might-be witches as did Princess Anne.

Grace Sherwood's alleged crime was that of bewitching county resident Elizabeth Hill and causing her to miscarry, in essence the murdering of Mistress Hill's unborn child. Although conviction as a witch in itself warranted the death penalty, this was a charge far more serious than the accusations of Jane Gisborne or Elizabeth Barnes, who claimed only the death of a pig and being ridden in the night.

Following the guidelines published by Dalton, the Princess Anne County authorities were ordered by the colony's General Court to empanel a female jury to search Grace Sherwood's house for incriminating images either waxen or perhaps fashioned from rye meal mixed with urine like those Tituba had baked in Salem Village. There was, however, no rush to join the jury, nor was there when a second distaff panel was ordered to examine Grace herself for the demon-suckling teats "not usual in Others" that would confirm that she was indeed a witch.

Having failed to empanel the teat-seeking jury, the county justices gave the order for Grace to be ducked to see whether or not she would float and thus provide the prosecution with the evidence it needed. The test was to be performed on July 5, 1706, but that being a wet day, it was postponed until the tenth!

The magistrates evidently were aware that the ducking procedure had its shortcomings and that no matter what the law allowed, drowning an innocent woman was not an option they wished to espouse. Consequently, they were at pains to instruct the searchers to take care to preserve Grace from drowning—a caveat that proved irrelevant. Though bound thumb to toe, Grace Sherwood floated.

Prior to her ordeal, the sheriff was to "request as many Ansient and Knowing women as possible . . . to Serch her Carefully For all teats spots and marks about her body . . . and further it [was] ord' that Som women be requested to Shift and Serch her before She goe into the water, that she Carry nothing about her to cause any Further Suspicion."

Grace's reluctance to sink was perceived by the throng of watchers to confirm her guilt, thereby emboldening several women to come forward to search for additional proof. And they found it. Upon her private parts they discovered, or said they did, "two things like titts," black in color. That was proof enough. Grace Sherwood was ordered to be clapped in irons and lodged in the "Common Gaol" to await trial.

What happened next is no longer known—as Colonial Williamsburg's reenactors make clear. Like so much of history, the crucial bit—the trial transcript—does not survive. It seems likely, however, that more educated thinking prevailed and that Grace Sherwood was acquitted or set free after having endured the ducking that was the prescribed punishment for "brabling women [who] slander and scandalize their neighbors." The will of a widow named Grace Sherwood was probated on October 1, 1740—when Grace, the presumably reformed witch, would have been about eighty years old. No known stone marks her grave and no state marker recalls her ordeal, but Witch Duck Road even now leads to Witch Duck Point. Across from it, on the west shore of Lynnhaven Bay, and still marked on some maps, stood the 1644–1735 courthouse that Grace Sherwood had known all too well.

As late as 1736 Virginia's justices of the peace were reminded that witchcraft was still a crime, but that first offenders could expect to be pilloried quarterly and be jailed for only a year. As for repeat offenders, they would do so but once. However, the

1738 edition of Ephraim Chambers's *Cyclopaedia* spoke to a more enlightened generation:

> Sorcery [the crime of witchcraft] was a thing formerly very common; at least the credulity of those ages made it pass for such; and people suffered frequently for it. In a more knowing and less believing age, it is out of doors.
>
> In effect, the most probable opinion is, that the several glaring instances of sorcery we meet withal, in our old law-books and historians, if well inquired into, would be found, at bottom, no other than artful poisonings.

But neither in eighteenth-century Virginia nor in England did rural folk read encyclopedias. The old ways, the old fears, lingered on—and on. Old women misshapen by age still told fortunes and threatened their neighbors with predicted calamities that sometimes proved true. But over time there came to be more white witches than black, more "wise women" than the "secret, black, and midnight hats" of Shakespeare's imagination. Nevertheless, when Halloween comes around, the modern witches of Salem take to their broomsticks and strange cries are heard in the night. For our part, many of us still hang horseshoes over our doors for luck—although, as one Jamestown deponent explained, horseshoes had other sorcery-related uses.

In 1626 Isabell Perry had accused Joan Wright of Surry County of being a witch, and in her testimony Mrs. Perry repeated at tiresome length what Goody Wright had told her about an experience she had had in England. While Joan worked as a servant to an unnamed "dame," her employer had fallen ill and believed that she was bewitched. Consequently, Joan was given the following instructions:

> That at the cominge of a woman, wch was suspected, to take a horshwe [horseshoe] and flinge it into the oven and when it was red hott, To fflinge it into her dames urine, and so long as the horshwe was hott the witch was sick at the harte, And when the Irone was colde she was well again. . . .

The casting of counterspells was common, and even essential to the well-being of sorcery's victims, and in its various forms continued much later than one might expect. In the third quarter of the seventeenth century provincial England was still reeling from the impact of Mathew Hopkins, the self-styled "Witch Finder General," who in the space of eighteen months discovered more than 200 witches, of whom 100 were executed. "Every old woman with a wrinkled face, a furrowed brow, a hairy lip, a tooth, a squint eye, a squeaking voice, or a scolding tongue . . . and a dog or cat at her side, is not only suspected but pronounced a witch," wrote skeptic and Puritan minister John Gaule in 1646. A few months later Hopkins would himself be accused of witchcraft, and according to one account drowned while being put to the swimming test.

Whatever the truth of Hopkins's death, the fear and suspicion he had generated lived on. Perhaps because his "Discoveries" were made in England's eastern counties of Essex, Norfolk, and Suffolk, it is there that most of the tangible evidence of antiwitch insurance has been found. At least fifteen Rhenish stoneware bottles (commonly called "Bellarmines" or "Grey-beards") have been found buried under the hearths of East Anglian houses.

Just as red-hot horseshoes were thrown into the victim's urine, the bottles were filled with iron nails, bent pins, and spikes from blackthorn bushes, and topped up with the urine. The theory had it that the witch (or her familiar) would come down to the pins, thorns, and nails. In some instances, the pins were thrust through a cutout cloth heart, presumably to ensure that they speared the right target. Why the pins were bent double remains anyone's guess. Mine is that the act of so doing was symbolic of the pain being "bent" back against the perpetrator.

As for the urine, Joseph Blagrave, writing in 1671 *(Astrological Practise of Physick),* explained it in this way: "The reason . . . is because there is part of the vital spirit of the Witch in it, for such is the subtlety of the Devil, that he will not suffer the Witch to infuse any poysonous matter into the body of man or beast, without some of the Witches blood mingling with it." For that reason, therefore, by capturing her blood in the bottle,

At the Wythe House kitchen, candles, it is said, sometimes travel from window to table without corporeal help.

The duty officer told her: "Rather you than me." He said that when it was his turn to patrol the building, he got in and out as fast as he could. He had sensed a presence on the stairs.

Standing in the darkness at their foot, I could well believe it. Two small patches of moonlight cast through the transom over the front door left a vertical bluish-gray streak between them that waxed and waned as clouds moved across the sky. That impression vanished as soon as Tanya lit a hallway candle whose flickering flame cast its own shadows up the staircase wall.

Meanwhile, with a powerful, ghost-dispelling flashlight, I helped Dave unpack his photographic equipment. That done, I set myself up in the second floor's southwest room and by the light of a single candle began to write down everything I saw and heard. It was fifteen minutes to midnight.

At 11:55 I heard a faint and eerily wailing sound—the voice of a distant ambulance speeding about its business on the other side of town. All else was silence save for the hum of the heating system. Its ceiling-fed air was causing my candle to waver in fluctuating spasms. Shadows of chair backs moved from side to side along the white walls. And somewhere in the darkness beyond the open door I could hear movement. But whether it was Dave setting up or Tanya moving about the building. . . .

I persuaded myself that it had to be one or the other.

Downstairs in the parlor Dave was standing in the darkness considering how best to set up his infrared camera when he saw a pale white shape in the corner. It became clearer as his eyes grew accustomed to the dark. It was a ceramic teapot on a cupboard shelf. It seemed to be alive with light. But it gave off none, leaving the other tea wares on the shelf in deep darkness. Of the ghostly experiences in the Wythe House, the ghostly teapot would cap them all—and Dave was there to record it on film.

Alas, there was a simple explanation. A small, circular peephole in the closed shutters let in a soft shaft of moonlight that fell on the teapot.

At my station upstairs, I was unaware of Dave's teapot drama. I had expected that somewhere in the house a clock would strike the midnight hour, but none did, and it was five minutes after before I again checked my watch. The plan was to remain in the house for another hour, and so I decided to first make my way down to the basement for a cup of adrenaline-boosting coffee. My all-powerful flashlight would show me the way. But when I switched it on, nothing happened. Its brand-new battery was dead.

Shortly after returning from the basement—aided by Tanya's flashlight—and settling back onto my chair, I felt a slowly growing chill down the back of my neck. Don't move, I told myself. Let whatever is happening, happen.

Nothing did. The thermometer in the room continued to read 71° F, and I had to conclude that the sensation was the product of body heat elevated by the coffee in conflict with draft from the heating system. Remembering my stepdaughter's experience in the Wythe kitchen, I sat staring fixedly at the candlestick willing it to move. It was now 12:45 a.m.

"If nothing happens in the next fifteen minutes," I wrote in my journal, "the spirits will have missed their golden opportunity, and the folks who have insisted that there are no ghosts in the Wythe House will nod sagely and say to each other, 'We told him so.'"

At 12:50 a.m. I wrote: "Time to pack up and leave the ghosts to their own amusements—at our expense." And so we did, remaining only long enough for Tanya Wilson to close the silent building. When she got up to go to work that morning, her car wouldn't start. Its battery was dead.

The next day, a lifelong resident of Williamsburg now in her eighties called to ask how we had fared in our vigil. When I confessed that nothing had happened, she said, "Of course not. You can't expect anything like that to happen to order, and certainly not with a photographer around. I know there are ghosts," she said. "You should try again—but do it on your own."

I don't think so.

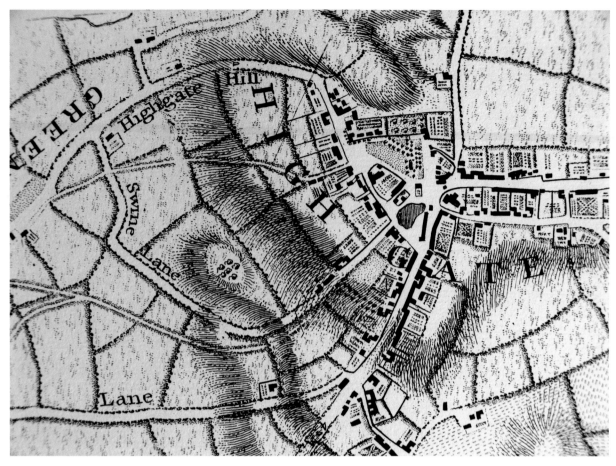

Detail of Highgate, from John Rocque's 1741 map of London, which shows where the chicken crossed the road.

Sir Francis and the Phantom Chicken

Sir Francis Bacon's name might not be well known in Williamsburg were it not for the belief of some individuals that he wrote Shakespeare's plays and had them buried in the churchyard of Bruton Parish. Not much better remembered is his kinsman Colonel Nathaniel Bacon of York County, credited in the same quarters with bringing the Shakespeare manuscripts from England. More important, and with much more certainty, he promoted his ne'er-do-well nephew, another Nathaniel, whose 1676 rebellion against Virginia's Governor William Berkeley shook the colony to its roots.

By coincidence or heredity, Nathaniel the Rebel's character bore a close resemblance to that of his illustrious forebear, variously described as being of an "ominous, pensive, melancholy aspect," leaning toward atheism, and of a "most imperious and dangerous hidden pride of heart, despising the wisest of his neighbors for their ignorance, and very ambitious and arrogant." A spendthrift and wheeler-dealer who contrived to swindle a friend out of his inheritance, Nathaniel was unwelcome enough at home that his father shipped him to Virginia in the care of his wealthy, land-owning uncle.

This, however, is the story of Nathaniel's more distant relation, Sir Francis Bacon, Baron Verulam and Viscount St. Albans, whose intellectual brilliance belied an arrogance and meanness of spirit in his pursuit of power and prominence.

Francis Bacon was born in London in 1561, the youngest of eight children who suffered the disapproval of a domineering Calvinist mother. Today, defense lawyers might argue that Francis's life was

scarred by a childhood of mental abuse and that winning the approval of his peers would become an obsession.

In 1573, Bacon and his elder brother Anthony entered Trinity College, Cambridge. They went on to read law at Grey's Inn. Bacon was called to the bar in 1582. Although only twenty-one, he had concluded that his philosophy teachers were hopelessly out of date, clinging to old and often baseless tenets. The thought process, Bacon said, should be grounded in fact rather than in theory, and the amassing of verifiable data should be the foundation for all such teaching. In 1605, at midlife, he would put all this into the treatise he titled *The Advancement of Learning*. It was, however, the advancement of Francis Bacon that occupied much of his attention.

Bacon's Calvinist upbringing made him a virulent anti-Catholic. Since 1570 it had been law that Catholics who refused to attend the Church of England—recusants—were to be prosecuted, but Bacon believed that could drive them underground and make them harder to control. He proposed a replacement law requiring those who refused to take up arms on the nation's behalf against the pope or other foreign foe to be condemned as traitors. In short, his proposal substituted patriotism for recusancy. It was not, however, the approach favored by the queen or her Parliament, and Bacon's 1584 proposal, laid out in "A Letter of Advice to Queen Elizabeth," did him no good. Then, as now, an unsolicited memo to the boss offering unpalatable advice was not a safe career move.

The letter was written soon after Bacon was elected to Parliament, probably in the realization that limiting his input to instantly forgotten speeches in the Commons would get him nowhere. If he was to have influence, it had to be sought where the power really resided, namely in the court and person of the queen. The obvious avenue was through Secretary of State Cecil

Lord Burghley, who had married his mother's sister. Although Uncle Cecil's initial response had been to ignore him, he helped Bacon secure his seat in Parliament and saw merit in him as a lawyer. But Bacon wanted more. He needed the ear of the queen.

In the sixteenth century the hub of government rotated around the axle of the monarch. It was an age of king worship, or in Bacon's case, queen worship. This was not despotism. It took no armies to stay in power. Indeed, the attitude of the people resembled that of America in the wake of the September 11 attack. The ruler was right and the populace was content to go along—even if some royal decisions were less applauded than others. On at least two parliamentary occasions Bacon's voice rose in opposition to the queen's wishes—particularly in respect to taxes and royal subsidies. For that he paid dearly. Elizabeth refused to see him, and, when his name was put forward for preferment, she turned him down. When asked why he took positions contrary to his best interests, Bacon said that conscience and expedience were not interchangeable.

During the years of royal disfavor Bacon found a potential new friend in a high place, the young, impetuous, enticingly rich, and ultimately incompetent Robert Devereux, second Earl of Essex. The epitome of his age, Essex was a courtier flamboyant in attire, a writer of sonnets, and a man strikingly handsome. Francis Bacon, as it happened, was drawn to young men who were handsome. Another such was his friend Sir John Danvers, who was described as "so beautiful and fine that people would come after him in the street to admire him." Seventeenth-century biographer John Aubrey put it bluntly: Bacon was a homosexual whose "Ganymedes and favorites" were open to bribery—as he, too, would prove to be. Nevertheless, like many another, Bacon would marry, choosing Frances Barnham, the daughter of a London alderman. She would outlive him by twenty years and marry Sir Thomas Underhill, whom, according to Aubrey, "she made deaf and blind with too much of Venus." It seems reasonable to deduce, therefore, that the childless Bacon marriage had not been one of faultless fidelity.

The intellectual relationship between Francis and Essex was of master and student or, to be

Bacon alternately wooed and lost Queen Elizabeth's favor.

more precise, puppet master and doll. Bacon saw an opportunity in the young man to mold him to his will and to keep his protégé's strings tightly knotted to his fingertips. Like most of Elizabeth's favorite courtiers, Robert Devereux was a man of action who demonstrated his loyalty by naval adventures against the hated Spaniards. His capture of Cadiz in 1595 made him a hero among his men but backfired at court, where the queen, who had no standing army, feared that he might pose a threat. Knowing this, Bacon coached Essex in the art of flattery. Essex persuaded Elizabeth he had no further military ambitions nor any desire to court populist favor—

although master and puppet knew better.

It would slowly become apparent to Bacon that the impetuous Essex was unlikely to mature into the malleable statesman whose every utterance could be guided and controlled. With problems in an unruly Ireland much on the national mind, Bacon suggested to Essex that a stint there might give him the kind of military exploits he craved, and at the same time get him out of England. Essex warmed to the idea, and so did the queen. In 1599, with much of Ireland in rebellion, Essex took to the field, or rather numerous fields, marching hither and thither and accomplishing little. Parliament called on him to return to England, but Elizabeth told him that he was not to until he had defeated the powerful Earl of Tyrone. Infuriated, Essex threatened to return to England with 3,000 men to make his presence felt in some undefined manner. He soon regretted his outburst, however, and hastily sailed for England in the hope of preempting any accusations of disloyalty that his enemies might make against him. Instead, he was brought to trial and faced, among others, the queen's learned counselor, Francis Bacon.

To Essex's dismay, his old friend and mentor testified against him and denied that he had been instrumental in sending him to Ireland. Bacon later justified his betrayal by explaining that it put him in a more favorable light with the queen and in a better position to intercede on Essex's behalf. The earl failed to see logic in this duplicity and was unpersuaded by Bacon's assurance that he loved few people more than he did Essex, "both for gratitude's sake and for your own virtues." Bacon had reason to be grateful. Essex had made forceful yet failing efforts to advance him and gave him a sizable estate in Twickenham Park, which Bacon at first piously refused. No less generous to his friends, and prone to living a life that they could better afford, he would later sell the estate for £1,800.

Essex got off with what amounted to a reprimand, was banned from court, and embarked on his last ill-conceived adventure. He would forcibly remove ministers who opposed him and place himself as the queen's premier advisor—though at their last meeting the queen had slapped him around the ear and told him never to return. On February 8, 1601, Essex assembled about 200 supporters and marched into London, calling on the City to rally to his banner. But the City sat on its hands; Essex was arrested, and once again the old friends faced each other, Bacon from the prosecution's bench and Essex from the dock. The trial was brief, and the outcome never in doubt. Found guilty on February 19, on the twenty-fifth the second Earl of Essex parted with his handsome head.

The queen's long reign was drawing to an end, and Bacon and many another counselor were trying to position themselves in the right direction when the winds of change blew down from Scotland. Queen Elizabeth I died March 23, 1603, and Bacon was quick to pledge his allegiance to the new king, James, and to offer his services in building rapport between the Scottish monarch and his entourage of uncultured advisors and his new and mostly reluctant English subjects. For this thoughtfulness, Bacon was granted a knighthood—albeit along with 300 others.

Further advancement came slowly, but come it did. In 1607, he was made solicitor-general, and while holding that office Bacon exhibited his talent for behind-the-scenes manipulation. In 1615, while prosecuting an old clergyman named Edmund Peacham on a charge of preaching treason, Bacon ordered him tortured. When that proved unsuccessful, Bacon lobbied privately with each judge of the King's Bench to secure a conviction. Three years later, he voted for the execution of Sir Walter Ralegh. Longtime friend Dr. William Harvey described Bacon as having the eye of a viper. Another contemporary called him "the wisest, brightest, meanest of mankind."

Between 1616 and 1618, Bacon's political and judicial fortunes flourished: first a privy-counselor, then lord keeper, and finally lord chancellor of England and a peerage as Lord Verulam. His title reflected his residence at Gorhambury, close to the site of Roman St. Albans, the town they had named Verulamium. His crest and badge being a boar, it was no exaggeration to say that Bacon was in hog heaven. He had inherited Gorhambury indirectly from his father, Sir Nicholas, enlarging an already substantial "Gothic" house into a mansion fit for a lord, if not for a king. According to Aubrey, when his lordship was in residence, it "seemed as if the

FOUNDATIONS
UNEARTHED

BY
MARIA BAUER

Maria Bauer's 1940 book argued a deep and knotted tale of hidden treasure: the papers of Francis Bacon, including proof of his authorship of Shakespeare's plays, lay buried in a vault beneath Bruton Parish churchyard.

court was there, so nobly did he live."

Not content with one house, Bacon built another about a mile distant across a park avenued with planted trees. Verulam House, as it was called, was an elaborate Italianate folly built around a central chimney stack into which all the fireplaces fed. There were two bathing rooms, and the kitchens, larders, and other support facilities were all below ground. Salon doors were painted with life-sized figures of classical gods. The windows of an upper room provided a grand prospect across the park, and on the opposite wall large mirrors provided a retro-image of the same view. As the master of Verulam House was wont to point out, "One should have seats for summer and winter, as well as clothes." The house cost £10,000 to build, but in 1666 it was sold for £400 to two St. Albans carpenters, who tore

it down and disposed of the lumber for as much again.

In 1621, Bacon reached his political and social pinnacle, being made Viscount St. Albans. But it was in that year, too, that his long winter began. Charged with taking bribes from suitors appearing in his courts, he was tried in the House of Lords and offered no defense other than that the gifts he had accepted did not affect his judicial judgments. Briefly imprisoned in the Tower of London, he was later pardoned by the king but never again allowed to appear in Parliament or to practice before the bar.

Bacon would live out the remaining five years of his life at Gorhambury. Pursued by creditors, and bereft of servants, who decamped, as he said, "like the flying of the vermin when the house is falling," he busied himself with philosophical studies. To remaining friends he expressed the wish that he had devoted his life to science rather than to the law and its fleeting fortunes. That he lacked the educational base he had so long ago espoused in his *Advancement of Learning* did not occur to him.

In his retirement, Bacon completed a history of Henry VII and began work on Henry VIII, but there is no evidence that he saw either as subjects for Shakespearian-style plays. It is true that, like so many others of his age, he tried his hand at poetry, and it is also true that at one time or another he was friends with the likes of playwright Ben Jonson; but it was another Bacon, American author Delia Bacon, who, in 1859, first promoted her namesake as one among several who had masqueraded under the name of Shakespeare. Delia has been described as "eloquent but almost insane," but three times in the twentieth century subscribers to her idea probed the Williamsburg churchyard for buried manuscripts. None turned up, but not everyone is persuaded there are none to be found.

Francis, too, had moments that made his friends and servants wonder. He was given to fainting fits and had a finely focused sense of smell. None of his servants dared face him unless wearing Spanish leather boots—the odor of any others offended him—and at every meal he ordered the table strewn with the season's flowers in the belief that they could refresh "his spirits and memory." Confident that his every thought could be a gem, Bacon liked

Drawn in the 1730s, the rendering of St. George's, Williamsburg's sister city in Bermuda, shows every identifiable window being glazed with casements rather than sash frames. Archaeological evidence from Williamsburg suggests that in the same period the city may have possessed more leaded windows than is often supposed. The painting, left, by an unidentified artist, of an English country house of the 1740s shows it to have been fitted with sash windows throughout its three main floors, but its small attic dormers were provided with greater airflow by means of fully opening casements. Though larger, this, the home of William Acton at Wolverton in Worcestershire, is of similar character to Virginia's own Rosewell in Gloucester County.

many Negro and Indian slaves"—10,000 as against Williamsburg's 1,500 nearly a hundred years later. By Port Royal standards, therefore, colonial Williamsburg was a very small town, indeed little more than an English village—where leaded casement windows survived well into the nineteenth century and some even to this day.

We may reasonably ask, therefore, why Whiffen believed that in Williamsburg "it is likely that they [sash windows] were universal in the homes of private houses of Williamsburg from the first."

Archaeological evidence paints a very different picture. But to understand that evidence, one must first know how casement windows were made and, by extension, what parts of them have remained for archaeologists to unearth.

Construction involved four separate crafts, those of blacksmithing for the iron frames, joinery to make the wooden frames to which the iron sometimes was nailed, glazing to cut the sheets of glass to panes (called quarrels) to the desired shape and size, and the lead working to cast and draw out the lead strips into which the quarrels were secured. Of these four trades, all but the first frequently were performed by the same artisan.

The lead was first cast into foot-long, H-sectioned bars known as cames, which were then pushed and pulled through a glazier's vise, the juxtaposition of whose wheels determined the thickness (and length) of the emerging turned lead. More often than not, however, the end product is incorrectly called a came.

The wheels of the glazier's vises were notched so that they could impart tiny ridges along the spines of the turned lead, this a device to help secure the glass in place. Sometimes, however, the vise maker engraved his name and date on the edges of the wheels so that this, too, could be transferred to the spines. The earliest example yet known was excavated in Martin's Hundred and dated 1625, while one of the latest was found at the great Elizabethan mansion Kirby Hall in England's Northamptonshire and dated 1733. Here, therefore, was evidence that even at that late date, old houses were having new leaded windows installed instead of replacing them with sashes.

By cutting and soldering the lead strips, an in-finite variety of designs was possible. Walter Gidde, in his 1615 *A Booke of Svndry Dravghtes, Principaly Serving for Glasiers: and not Impertinent for Plasterers and Gardiners,* illustrated 103 separate window compositions. As a rule, however, purely functional windows were limited to cutting the glass into squares, rectangles, and most often diamond shapes. As late as 1736 Richard Neve's *City and Country Purchaser' and Builder's Dictionary* (3rd edition) devoted most of its section on glazing to describing and pricing work related to casements and to diamond-shaped and square "quarries."

In the early days of window-glass manufacturing, the mix was the same as that used to blow green-glass bottles and drinking vessels, and so, no matter how thin the sheets, their greenish color and unevenness of surface ensured that their optical qualities were minimal. For that reason the cut panes were small, and it was not until a means was found to overcome those problems that panes became larger and rendered practical the making of sash windows. But like any new product, the larger panes were more expensive, and so home owners who already had their houses fitted with casements continued to do so, replacing broken quarrels with new. Since many of those window openings were not suited to the installation of pulley systems, home owners replaced the old leaded casements with new glazing bars and larger panes set in hinged wooden frames that continued to open outward.

Window glass was made in two ways, one known as the muff method of making broad glass, the other the crown process. The former involved blowing an elongated glass bubble, cutting off both ends, laying the resulting tube onto an iron sheet in the furnace, and cutting the tube lengthwise, so that it could be reheated and rolled flat—or more or less flat. Crown glass, on the other hand, was made first by blowing the bubble, then attaching an iron rod to the end of it (called the pontil), freeing the bubble from the blowing iron and spinning it back and forth on the arms of the glassmaker's chair until it opened out into a disk, which could be as much as five feet in diameter. When these huge discs reached the glazier, he cut his best and largest panes from near the edge, then the smaller as the panes became increasingly thick, until they reached close to the optically useless green knob of the pontil. Although that central bull's-eye has long been thought cutely Olde Worlde, it generally was only used in panes mounted over door transoms or in the windows of cellars, where they served only to transmit light.

How, one might wonder, is it possible to tell the difference between a cut pane of crown glass and a fragment of broad glass? The answer lies primarily in their air bubbles. Those in broad glass are more or less spherical, while those in crown are elongated as the result of spinning the disk. Careful examination of the latter's panes will often show semicircular striations, and occasionally, when a pane has been cut too close to the outer edge, an abrupt thickening is found at one corner.

These, then, are the pieces of information we need to gauge the relevance of Williamsburg's historical and archaeological evidence.

Between October 1732 and April 1735, Wil-liamsburg carpenter James Wray worked on behalf of the then operator of the Raleigh Tavern, Henry Wetherburn, work that included, among eighteen glass-related entries, "Putting In 49 Diamond Panes of Glass," "18 foot of old Glass Sett in New Lead," "Mending a Light in an Iron Casement," and "Repairing 10 foot of old Glass." However, in a four-month period in late 1734 and early 1735, Wray also provided Wetherburn with "A Bottom Rail to a Sash" and nine "Sash Panes."

If we are safe in concluding that the entries marked "To the Account of work Done at Mr. Wetherburn" related to the Raleigh, they are telling us that by 1734, if no earlier, the tavern possessed both casement and sash windows. If so, it is highly likely that the latter were installed in its principal first floor rooms and that the attic or bedroom floor retained out-opening, diamond-quarreled casements.

One has only to look at the attic dormers of restored Williamsburg buildings to see how narrow

Leaded casement windows like these, reconstructed from fragments found in the cellar of a house now covered by Nassau Street, must have given Williamsburg's early houses a very different appearance from those we see today.

English artists like James Gillray, William Hogarth, and Thomas Rowlandson saw leaded casement windows as giving scenic character to tenements and taverns. The detail from Gillray's 1806 cartoon against increased property taxes, *right*, shows not only such windows but also a Williamsburg-style bird bottle. Hogarth's 1755 An Election Entertainment, *below*, allows slops to go out and much-needed fresh air to flow in through the inn's casement windows.

out of a total colonial population of about 1,400.

The identification of diseases in the early seventeenth century—and later for that matter—is difficult, the term "plague" being used in its loosest terms. Thus John Smith in his 1624 *Generall Historie* wrote that in New England Captain Miles Standish had visited the Cape Cod village of Manomet, "where the people had the plague, a place much frequented with Dutch and French." However, colonist Edward Winslow in his pamphlet *Good Newes from New-England* (1624) described the same incident and called the outbreak only "a great sickness."

That the colonies experienced many a contagious disease there can be no doubt; nevertheless, it may seem surprising that in the early eighteenth century a Virginian should write *A Discourse Concerning the Plague, with some preservatives Against it*—until one discovers the nature of the preservatives. The author, who modestly called himself "A Lover of Mankind," seems to have been that busy diarist, poet, songwriter, bon viveur, lone dancer, and attentive master to his white maid Annie, William

Byrd II of Westover. A voracious reader in Latin, Hebrew, and Greek, he also fancied himself an amateur physician who, at the drop of a cough, would prescribe for his friends and workers an appropriate physick.

Although there is no confirmation that Byrd was the "Lover of Mankind" who published his thesis in London in 1721, entries in his diary are strongly suggestive. On February 24 he wrote that "I danced my dance and then wrote some English about the plague." By mid-March the writings had become "my book fair about the plague," and six days later it was finished. On this, the twenty-second, Byrd recalled that after lunch (then called dinner) he "walked to Mrs. Harrison's [at Berkeley Plantation] where I read over my book and she liked it very much."

The treatise, which has much to say about vomiting and smells so foul that a nose blocked and a mouth filled with vinegar-soaked sponges could not escape it, would seem to have been a less than enjoyable after-lunch experience for the widowed

The London Fire of 1666 destroyed much of the city and may have killed enough of its flea-bearing rats to create a fifty-four-year interruption in the cycle of plague epidemics. The author of the Discourse, *however, attributed the relief to "the universal use of Tobacco."*

Mrs. Harrison. Indeed, one can imagine her, face half-hidden behind her fan, mumbling flatly, "Very nice, Mr. Byrd—and so different."

Four days later Colonel Harrison came to Westover for breakfast and suffered the same fate. Wrote Byrd, "I read some of my plague book to him." What Harrison thought of it went unrecorded and probably unspoken. On April 4, Byrd gave to the captain of an England-bound ship "my letters and my book about the plague to deliver to Mr. Perry."

Micajah Perry was a wealthy, ship-owning London merchant who served as agent for several prominent Virginia planters. It seems likely, therefore, that Byrd asked him to find a printer for his plague treatise, for, as previously noted, the pamphlet was published in the same year—price one shilling.

William Byrd's friends and neighbors may have breathed a sigh of relief when they heard that the manuscript had been shipped to England. But it would have been short-lived. He had another copy. Four days later Westover Church's Huguenot minister Peter Fontaine spent the night at the plantation, providing Byrd with a heaven-sent opportunity to "read [his] book to him about the plague."

The forty-page booklet is as much a promotional tract for the plague-avoiding properties of tobacco as it is an amateur's contribution to the corpus of epidemiological medicine. Wrote Byrd:

In England it [the plague] used formerly to make a visit about once in twenty or thirty years: but since the universal use of Tobacco, it has now been kept off above fifty four years. Without the assistance of the powerful Alexipharmick, it were, humanly speaking, impossible to have warded it off so long.

He omitted to note that the English—man, wife, widow, and boy—had been smoking like chimneys throughout the first sixty-four years of the century that preceded the disaster. He also omitted to note that others believed the Great Fire that swept through London in 1666 had done much to cleanse it of plague-bearing rats.

Before embarking on a lengthy dissertation on what to do with tobacco—both to cure and prevent the plague—Byrd did allow that unless properly used tobacco could be injurious to one's health. "Tobacco is truly a poison," he wrote. "The chymical oil of it will kill all animals, from a Louse up to an Elephant. The very smoak of it will both purge and vomit; and 'tis so very penetrating, that the infusion will do the same thing, if outwardly applied to the stomach and navel."

These bothersome side effects seemed to be of small concern to Byrd, who ended his "book" with propositions guaranteed to promote happiness down the ages to the tobacco—if not to the pharmaceutical—industry. At the first hint of pestilence one couldn't do better than to provide oneself "with a reasonable quantity of fresh, strong scented Tobacco."

We shou'd wear it about our clothes, and about our coaches. We should hang bundles of it around our beds, and in the apartments wherein we most converse. If we have an aversion to smoking, it would be very prudent to burn some leaves of Tobacco in our dining rooms, lest we swallow the infection with our meat. It will also be very useful

to take snuff plentifully made of the pure leaf, to secure the passages to our brain. Nor must those only be guarded, but the pass to our stomachs should be also safely defended.

How? one might naively inquire.

With chewing tobacco, replied Byrd, who, as it happened, grew and could supply vast quantities of "this great *Antipoison!*"

To be fair to Byrd, one has to allow that his researches had led him down several preventative avenues, albeit further down some than others.

The government of any stricken land should call for a general fasting and a great deal of potent prayer, advised Byrd, also "profaneness and immorality [should be] severely punished"—to which Annie would almost certainly have whispered, "Amen to that!" Byrd went on to declare that "we should keep our spirits chearful and erect."

"A terrify'd and dejected mind," he insisted, "will dispose us most unaccountably to suck in the very distemper we are afraid of." He ended by urging that, when all else failed, prayer would be both a first and last resort. "Let us therefore cast ourselves before his throne, sadly confessing our sins, and deprecating his just vengeance . . . intercede for our dear Country, entreating his tender mercy to save those that are already sick, and preserve those that are well from the infection."

The odd thing about all this was, as Byrd himself admitted, that there hadn't been an outbreak of bubonic plague in England for half a century. So why did he write his book?

Or *did* he write the book?

Quite clearly and deliberately, the text is written to imply that the work is by an Englishman—hence the intercession for "our dear Country"—and by someone resident in London. Thus, in writing about the plague of 1665, the author refers to the loss of "so many thousand Souls in this city" and, later, to "so terrible a massacre here at London." However, William Byrd was England bound and may well have been there by the time the treatise came from the printer. Besides, outside the captive Harrisons and the vicar—and maybe the long-suffering Annie—the readership for even a shortish book on a disease unknown in America would have been a slow seller in Williamsburg. So it could best have been penned with the English market specifically in mind and seemingly by an Englishman who knew whereof he wrote. Accepting the presumption that William Byrd wrote it, why did he do so?

The answer is to be found in a letter Byrd received on February 14, 1721, only six days before he began to pen "some English concerning the plague." The unnamed correspondent writing from England advised him "that the plague was there." This, of course, belies the assurance that, thanks to the use of good Virginia tobacco, the plague had not been diagnosed in England in the past half-century. It is undeniable, however, that the plague had broken out in the Levant and that it spread across Europe to the port of Marseilles early in 1721. Being a readily ship-borne disease, it caused fear and consternation in England, prompting the reprinting of tracts on the 1665 outbreak and the publication of other helpful or fear-promoting pamphlets besides Byrd's.

He was in most excellent company. For even as Byrd was powdering his ink at Westover, Daniel Defoe in London was at work on one of the greatest pieces of reconstructive reporting in all of English literature: his *A Journal of the Plague Year,* which retold the story of the 1665 outbreak. In it Defoe did for the Great Plague what Samuel Pepys in the added immediacy of his coded diaries had done for the Great Fire that was to follow in 1666.

William Byrd, of course, was not in the same league as Defoe or Pepys; nevertheless, and in the guise of helpful hints, here was a wordsmith of no little skill cleverly peddling both fear and his best Virginia leaf. Lest there should be any misunderstanding, the pamphlet's tailpiece illustration featured a dancing Indian wearing tobacco leaves where feathers usually were worn.

William Byrd was no stranger to disease. While in London his wife, Lucy Parke, had died of smallpox in 1716, and three years later his daughters Evelyn and Wilhelmina were thought to have contracted it. The latter actually did so, as the diary noted, "but very favorably." The following day, July 15, 1719, Byrd could write, "My little daughter was better, thank God."

Though by no means as virulent as the Black Death, smallpox was a communicable disease carried not by rat fleas or elevated through the air but by simple human contact. And it, too, was often called a plague. Thus in Scotland in 1610 the Kirk Records of Aberdeen reported that there had been "a great visitation of the young children with the plague of the pox." In 1722, the year after Byrd wrote his book, an outbreak in London resulted in more than 3,000 deaths. Although today that would be considered a major eruption, it paled beside the memory of the 68,000 deaths from the bubonic plague of 1665. Nevertheless, to William Byrd and his generation, the fear of contagious diseases was real, ever present, and, for those with a literary bent, worth writing about.

Besides, for tobacco planter Byrd, there was an even more alarming reality—that of falling tobacco prices, overproduction, and competition. But, if fear-filled English smokers and nonsmokers could be persuaded to wear it, wipe it, hang it, sniff it, and chew it—Well, did not God move in marvelous ways his wonders to perform?

Wearing tobacco leaves instead of feathers as a headdress, the naked Indian cherub ornament that marks the end of A Discourse Concerning the Plague *is more suggestive of the leafy preventative it recommends than the graphic horrors of the Black Death.*

FINIS

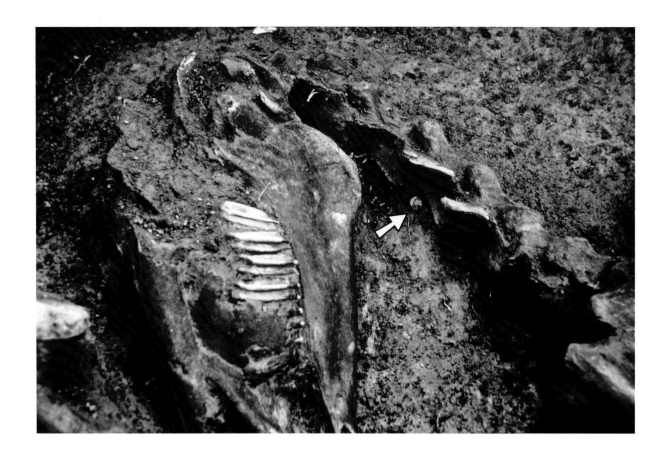

A Tale of Two Bullets

The victim lay dead in a ditch on Nicholson Street, shot squarely between the eyes. I would discover sometime later that there had been a second shot fired from a different gun.

On two occasions over the years I've been called in to assist the Williamsburg police. But this was different.

Historians have called May 5, 1862, a "brisk delaying action" and a "scrap at Williamsburg," as Confederate General Joseph E. Johnson withdrew from Yorktown to be followed by the ever-cautious Union commander General George B. McClellan. But it was more than that, much more.

A light but soaking rain had been falling on and off for days, and the roads of Williamsburg were a sea of mud, as caissons, artillery, supply wagons,

A round ball, arrowed, above, and a minie ball in the photo at right bore testimony to a tragedy common in the aftermath of every Civil War battle.

and cavalry trundled back and forth, some moving toward redoubts erected by Confederate General Magruder and others withdrawing to more defensible positions nearer Richmond.

The genteel ladies, children, and old men of the decaying and half-forgotten colonial capital listened to the distant rumble of artillery and watched with growing horror as the horse-drawn ambulances rattled into town laden with bloodied and groaning wounded. In the sodden fields and dripping woods barely a mile from town, the Battle of Williamsburg had begun.

With banners flying and voices cheering, 600 men of the 24th Virginia regiment charged out of the woods into the open toward General Hancock's five regiments, ten guns, and 4,000 waiting muskets. In spite of heavy losses, the 24th Virginia, helped by another 600 from the 5th North Carolina, came within a fence of overrunning the vastly outnumbering Union brigade—until the ill-informed Confederate General A. P. Hill ordered them to withdraw. In doing so, the day was lost, and the casualties mounted as "the foe, quickly rallying and reforming . . . hurled shot and shell through their devoted ranks with awful destruction."

An incredulous Hancock would dub the 24th Virginia the "Immortals."

Casualty numbers vary, but together the two armies are believed to have suffered about 774 killed and 2,417 wounded. Most of the injured flooded into Williamsburg to be billeted wherever a cot could be found. Adding to the terrified citizens' misery, before the day was out, their cherished little town would be in the hands of the hated Yankees—and would remain so for most of the war.

A hundred and three years later the trauma of the mud, the pain, the stench of death, and the garbage of war was unexpectedly brought into focus during archaeological work on Nicholson Street near the site of Anthony Hay's cabinet shop. In a ditch beside the old road that sloped much more steeply than it does today lay the skeleton of a small horse, its legs broken and bizarrely twisted.

How did it get there, and when?

In the best detective-story tradition, we found the killing bullet. It had been fired at short range through the animal's head and into the muscles of its neck. A round ball from a smooth-bore gun, it could just as well have been of colonial vintage. It remained to a second bullet to give us the date and a good idea of what had happened. Lodged in the horse's belly in front of its broken pelvis rested a minie ball—or, more correctly, the bullet perfected by James H. Burton at the Harper's Ferry Arsenal circa 1855. Although the Union and Confederate Armies both used the new rifle-musket, which at 1,000 yards could penetrate four inches of pine, many old smooth-bored, ball-firing muskets and pistols were employed by the Confederates throughout the war.

All the evidence pointed to the horse having been shot when, after the rout of the 24th Virginia, the Confederates retreated into and beyond Williamsburg. Unable to carry its rider further, the tired and wounded mount collapsed in the swale on Nicholson Street, where it was shot through the head by its owner. Later, when rigor mortis had rendered the carcass awkward to move, a clean-up crew broke its legs, rolled it down into the roadside ditch, and shoveled dirt over it.

Was another scenario possible? Well, yes.

In the aftermath of the battle, with Williamsburg under martial law and Union Colonel David Campbell its provost marshal, he and his garrison were kept on their toes by "small bodies of cavalry who dashed into the streets at any hour of the day or night, killing or capturing a picket or two, or dispersing both pickets and guards, holding brief conferences with groups of citizens and retiring as suddenly as they came." It is conceivable, therefore, that the horse paid the price for a Confederate cavalryman who lingered too long.

Either way, in our search for the eighteenth century, archaeology had stumbled upon a poignant moment in the continuing history of the town millions know only as Colonial Williamsburg.

Perhaps none of de Bry's engravings is more often reproduced than A Weroan or great Lorde of Virginia. *Shown here as it appeared in a 1590 German imprint—from which all but two of the drawings in this story were photographed—it depicts a member of an Algonquian tribe from the 1580s in what is now the North Carolina coast. Notice the bowmen in the background hunting a stag.*

Nothing Without Care
Engraver Theodore de Bry did his best in the selling of America

Long before Columbus set out across the Atlantic, Europeans knew that there was something out there. Norsemen Leif Ericsson and his father, Eric the Red, reached Greenland in A.D. 981 and founded a settlement on its fertile southwest shore. But both being the product of a cold clime, it probably never occurred to them that hot might be better. For all their legendary fame, however, they were by no means the first Europeans to sail in that direction. Iceland was reached by Irish monks around A.D. 790, and a hundred years later

Scandinavian explorers found it again, established a colony there, and called it New Norway. At the turn of the first Christian millennium, Ericsson landed his people on the northern tip of Newfoundland island, a location later known as L'Anse aux meadows. Had they gone a little further—and maybe they did—they would have been the first known Europeans to build on the American mainland. In any case, he saw it and called it Vinland.

Although the 160-strong company of colonists Ericsson left on the island was considerably larger

123

than those that would land at Jamestown and at the mouth of the Kennebec more than half a millennium later, the venture was not a success. At least three reinforcing attempts were made, the last succumbing after five years. The final failure was blamed in part on Ericsson's conniving half sister, Freydis, who got her way by dispatching all the opposing colonists' wives with her very own ax. The Norwegian settlements on Greenland, however, fared much better, remaining there well through the fifteenth century. We can be reasonably certain that by then, first Danes and then Breton and Basque fishermen knew of the wealth of cod to be caught off the Grand Banks of Labrador. The notion that Columbus sailed bravely off across the ocean blue uncertain whether he might slip off the edge is unfounded. That the world was a ball and not a floating Frisbee had been deduced by the beginning of the Middle Ages, and, in spite of the objections of conservative monks, Pope Sylvester II (999–1063) accepted the sphericity of the Earth. So, too, did the influential "doctor Miribilis," as the renowned English philosopher and scientist Friar Bacon (ca. 1214–92) was called.

Columbus, like so many after him, was sailing west to reach the East. Consequently, when he wound up at the ribbon of islands garlanding the Caribbean, contemporary logic dictated that they had to be the western edge of the Indies.

Although the Spaniards and Portuguese of the early sixteenth century did their best to keep their discoveries secret, courtiers, like modern legislators, were prone to leaking. By the time Francis Drake sailed his *Golden Hind* around the world and arrived home September 26, 1580, no cats were left in the bag. With Spain reaping the riches of Incan Peru and Aztec Mexico, the French and Dutch were looking hungrily westward. The New World land grab was

Their sitting at meate, *above, was captioned in part: "Their meate is Mayz sodden . . . of verye good taste, deers flesche, or of some other beaste, and fishe." Opposite top, A cheiff Ladye of Pomeiooc shows a woman and child who lived in a village twenty miles inland from the English fort on Roanoke Island. Canoeists fish in the background. An ageed manne in his winter garment, opposite bottom, presents a member of the same village—shown behind him.*

in high gear, and in Elizabethan England a handful of adventurers, mercantile and marauding, were
urging that their country shed its insularity and
commit men and money to the great adventure.

While the knighted Drake spent his time de-
stroying anything Spanish, Sir Walter Ralegh set
about building himself something English on the
American mainland. It turned out, of course, that
North Carolina's Roanoke Island was not an ideal
place to do that, and, after three failed attempts at
colonization, the slamming and locking of investors' coffers in London and Plymouth became dis-
concertingly loud. On returning from Roanoke in
1586, scientist Thomas Harriot had written a glow-
ing account of Ralegh's New-Found Land. More-
over, America's most dedicated promoter, Richard
Hakluyt, was rounding up every explorer's and
mariner's report for inclusion in his *Principal Navi-
gations Voyages Traffiques & Discoveries of the English
nation* to be published two years later. But, with the
threat of a Spanish invasion in the offing, seizing a
slice of America took a back stool.

Hakluyt's diligence and tenacity were praised.
But some moneymen shook their heads, though
they allowed that, "yea, verily 'tis a noble work,
Dick'n. But, hast thou not . . ." (bankers talked like
that in those days), "but, hast thou not some pretty
pictures to spark it up, withal?" And this was where
Theodore de Bry came in.

De Bry was born in 1528 in the Flemish city of
Liège but weaned a Huguenot—not a smart thing to
be when Catholic Spaniards were wreaking havoc
through the Netherlands. In 1570, therefore, at the
age of forty-two, and, as he said, "stripped of all be-
longings by accidents, cheats, and ill luck and the
depredation of robbers," de Bry fled to Strasbourg,
where he set himself up as a goldsmith. Because
few customers wanted gold with nothing written or drawn on it, he became a dab hand with an
engraver's burin. Art, he said, restored his wealth
and reputation "and has never failed me, its tireless
devotee."

Someone with the foresight of a modern Fogel
or a Nagel suggested to de Bry that a series of illustrated travel guides could be a sure way to make
a ducat. Almost from the outset of New World ex-
ploration, expeditions rarely put to sea without

someone aboard who could draw or paint, if only
well enough to demonstrate that they got there—
even if they weren't too sure where there was. As
early as 1548, a Hessian named Hans Staden had
been a crewman on a Portuguese ship bound for
Brazil, where he fell into the hands of cannibals.
The man-eaters thought him more interesting than
tasty, and before, or perhaps after, being rescued
two years later, Staden made drawings of tribes-
men and -women—particularly the women as they
prepared people for the pot. Converted into crude
woodcuts, Staden's pictures caused a modest sensation when published in 1557. De Bry believed that
Staden's narrative, reissued with superior, engraved

De Bry's conception of Florida Indians killing alligators comes from a brief sixteenth-century narrative of the Spanish territory. Opposite are his The true picture of a woman Picte *and* The true picture of one Picte.

illustrations, might make a best-seller.

But, while he worked on the Staden engravings, de Bry conceived a far more grandiose enterprise. The Brazilian adventure could be but a single chapter in a vast, fully illustrated publication that would bring together accounts of New World travels and discoveries by other adventurers and their artists. Thus was born de Bry's *Historia Americae,* which would run to fourteen volumes before it was finished.

The Huguenot French had established a foothold in Spanish Florida by building first Fort Charles and later Fort Caroline. The latter was seized by the Spaniards in 1565, at which time the French artist Jacques le Moyne de Morgues barely escaped with his life. Rather than return to a Catholic-dominated France, he went to London, there changing his name to James Morgues, and produced a set of fine watercolors of all that he had seen in Florida. Only one survives.

When de Bry learned of le Moyne's illustrations, he went to London and tried to buy them with a view to using them as a basis for engravings to illustrate the record of France's failed Floridian colony. But le Moyne refused to sell. After le Moyne's death, however, and with the help of Richard Hakluyt, de Bry obtained the pictures and used them as he had intended. There was a price to pay for Hakluyt's help. De Bry would have to place Harriot's report on the Roanoke project ahead of those of the French or the Spaniards.

Sir Richard Grenville led the first English attempt to settle Roanoke Island. He had taken with him artist John White, whose 1586 drawings of plant and marine life in the Caribbean and of the Secotan Indians inhabiting the mainland south of the island were just what de Bry needed. It has often been said that White remained with the 1585 colonists and returned with them to England in

1586, but it is this writer's opinion that his stay had been short-lived and that he had gone home with Grenville in the summer of 1585. Be that as it may, White's watercolors, now in the British Museum, provided de Bry with accurate renderings to be translated into high-quality copperplate engravings to illustrate Harriot's *A briefe and true report of the new found land of Virginia*. It was published in 1590 in English, French, German, and Latin.

In his dedication to Sir Walter Ralegh, de Bry somewhat ruefully allowed that his English friends had persuaded him to publish Harriot's report before the rest "by reasons of the late performance thereof, albeyt I have in hand the History of Florida which should be first set forth because it was discovered by the Frenchmen long before the discovery of Virginia." He said he hoped soon to have that history in print—and did in 1591. Then followed the gruesome Hans Staden story in the following year, its title page enriched with renderings of Indians broiling people parts and gnawing on arms and legs. This was, one might think, in deliberate contrast to the "noble savage" treatment afforded to the Roanoke title page.

There is no doubt the Protestant de Bry was pleased to serve as a propagandist for his English friends and against the Spaniards, who raped and pillaged his Flemish homeland. Thus, between 1594 and 1596, de Bry illustrated the narratives of Milanese Girolamo Benzoni, who in 1541 began a fifteen-year stint in the Spanish New World colonies and returned to detail their bestial treatment of the Indians. De Bry pulled no punches; he showed Spaniards watching as their mastiffs tore prisoners limb from limb, other Indians having their hands and feet cut off, and yet more being burned when they declined to reveal where gold was hidden.

As more and more became known about the indigenous inhabitants of the New World, archaeological scholars from London to the Vatican were seeing in their culture and their primitive tools parallels to the European's prehistoric millennia. After his 1585 visit to the Algonquian aborigines of North Carolina, John White subscribed to this growing antiquarian parallelism by drawing and painting his ideas of what an ancient Englishman and -woman might have looked like—with clothes of a sort—as well as a Pictish pair of painted Scots—without them. Whether this not-so-subtle difference reflected the current English attitude toward perceived barbarians still living on the wrong side of Hadrian's Wall remains a matter for not very useful speculation. It is clear, however, that were White alive today, he could make a killing as a tattoo artist.

Though White's prehistoric people had nothing to do with Harriot and the Roanoke ventures, de Bry redrew them. He said in his introduction to them that he had been given five paintings "for to showe how that the Inhabitants of the Great Bretannie have bin in times past as sauvage as those of Virginia." Strangely, however, the five surviving White paintings show two Pictish men and one woman and two supposed "ancient Britains." But de Bry engraved one Pictish male and two women. Although he credited all five to White, art historian Paul Hulton said the extra woman was copied from a miniature by le Moyne, suggesting, perhaps, that White copied all of them from the Frenchman. That, of course, doesn't explain why de Bry omitted the second male in favor of the admittedly more attractive female.

As luck would have it, in their day, de Bry's portrayals of "The Pictes which in the olde tyme dyd habite one part of great Bretainne" saw wider circulation than the Roanoke story. The naked Picts redrawn as "Portraitures and Painting of the Ancient Britains" and the attired Britons as "more civill Britains" were used to illustrate John Speed's massive *The Historie of Great Britaine*, which was published in 1611 and went into its third edition in 1632.

In 1597, a year before his death, de Bry engraved his own portrait, and, as he had throughout his illustrating life, he did his best to be truthful. We see him as an old man with vacant eyes that have spent too many years staring at graven copper. His hair is tousled, his moustache and beard untrimmed, and in his long-fingered, knotted, and bony hands he holds a pair of calipers and a human skull. Beneath this unflatteringly honest portrait are the words of his motto NVL SANS SOUCI, or, Nothing Without Care. A contemporary and friend, Jean-Jacques Boissard, said de Bry "delineates everything with such perfection, that a young man of thirty could not do it with more precision."

De Bry did not live to engrave plates for John Smith's vigorous narrative of his travels and history of Virginia, the first part of which would not be published until 1610. The de Bry family, however, was to continue the work until 1634 and would illustrate some of Smith's heroics, as well as a promotional plug for the bounty of New England. Perhaps because the English investors were satisfied that they needed no more promotional pictures to help sell lots, no artists of the caliber of le Moyne or White accompanied the settlers to Jamestown or to Plymouth. Consequently, the de Bry family renderings owed more to imagination than to fact.

Nothing can be more telling than the change of style between the 1590 title page for Harriot's narrative and that of the 1634 edition, which preceded the Jamestown-era series. In the 1590 publication the male and female Indians appear gentle, nubile, and decently robed. In the 1634 work they appear as naked monsters, the woman with breasts dangling to her navel, corn in one hand and a dead goose dangling by its neck from the other.

The most familiar of all the Virginia engravings

De Bry's vision of the Garden of Eden, opposite, serves as a frontispiece in his collection of Virginia engravings. The wildly fanciful rendition of the Virginia Massacre of 1622, above, is not the work of de Bry, but of one of his family.

was drawn in this degenerated de Bry era. It purports to illustrate the 1622 Indian massacre of the English settlements, and, although it may owe something to a now-lost woodcut from a broadside describing the attack, the action and buildings are fanciful. Behind the foreground mayhem, we see four canoes crammed with Indians rowing furiously toward the fortified James Towne, whose artillery batteries expel impressive balloons of smoke. No such river-borne attack is recorded, and the scene of colonists being dragged from their table-clothed breakfast almost certainly was

culled from Edward Waterhouse's 1622 text, *Relation of the Barbarous Massacre.* It told how "in some places [the Indians] sate downe at Breakfast with our people at their tables."

In 1906, when Lyon G. Tyler published his famed *The Cradle of the Republic,* he perpetuated the de Bry family myth by using a redrawing of the already fictional fortified township as his Jamestown frontispiece. Old Theodore's grand concept of this *Historia Americae, Les Grands et Petits Voyages,* deserves to be remembered by work far better than this. But such are the quirks of historical survival.

William Hogarth. 1764

The wastefulness of wealth is exemplified by the bric-a-brac in the foreground, the results of unwise bidding at an art auction, from Marriage à la Mode.

William Hogarth
Eighteenth-century Norman Rockwell

For many Americans of an older and gentler generation, Norman Rockwell was the mirror of the mid-twentieth century. His children, his old folks, his guys in a diner or in a barber shop make us look back with loving smiles. Nodding sagely, we assure latter-day skeptics, "Yep, that's the way it was back then. But of course you wouldn't understand. How could you?"

William Hogarth was, like Rockwell, a pictorial chronicler of a mid-century era, but there the similarity ends. Rockwell is remembered for his soft-hued brushwork; Hogarth for acid etching. To collectors of American colonial and British antiques, as well as to students of life in the eighteenth century, Hogarth's name is synonymous with photographic objectivity in the reigns of the first Hanoverian Georges. He was born in 1697 and engraved his last plate in 1764, six months before his death. Beginning as an apprentice silver engraver in 1712, he became the mirror of English social mores and looked with equal disdain on the paths to poverty or to political advancement.

In A Harlot's Progress, *left, Hogarth detailed the chattels of penurious death—medicine bottles and a broken mug on the mantle, among them.* The Distressed Poet, *right, shows that the life of the spouse of a literary man was not romantic.*

To many a museum curator, Hogarth's depictions of household furnishings have been the authenticating crutches for a period room. When we apply the myopic eye of the archaeologist to his *Marriage à la Mode,* painted in 1745, or his *Industry and Idleness,* from 1747, we find an immense array of objects. The mug and medicine vial on a mantle shelf, a cracked jar in a shadowed closet, or a pile of useless and damaged bric-a-brac from a successful, but ill-advised, art auction bid—all are there. So, too, are the mousetraps, paint pots, coal shovels, and threadbare britches in need of repair—every one drawn with a cataloger's precision. And then there are his wine bottles.

We find them on tables, under tables, on the floor, beside beds—providers of solace for mourners, fuel for harlots' bile, and ambrosia to fuddle the minds of voters and press-ganged simpletons.

Although the eighteenth century as Hogarth knew and recorded it covered more than sixty years, we are inclined to imagine it as all of a piece, and to assume that something he drew in 1730 would be the same when he engraved it again in 1760. This makes no more sense than expecting a Model A Ford of 1930 to look the same as a Dodge coupe of 1960.

In the course of Hogarth's working life the old guard of the Stuart Age died off as the Dutch

Glass bottles, from about 1685 to about 1745, in shapes Hogarth knew and drew

In A Midnight Modern Conversation, *left, and in a detail from* A Rake's Progress, *right, the artist drew short-stemmed drinking glasses with bowls that have been interpreted as hexagonal. Rare, they are by collectors called "Hogarth glasses."*

and Germans moved in. Baroque gave way to rococo, Queen Anne lost out to Chippendale, the blue of the dining table's delftware was slowly eclipsed by the stark whiteness of saltglaze, and, in its turn, saltglaze by the gaudiness of multihued cream-colored earthenware. Bottles, too, evolved.

The question is whether Hogarth responded to this evolution with the same fidelity with which he separated high from low life. Bottle shapes common in the early years of his career—circa 1722–35—began squat and broad based but grew steadily taller as the years passed. By the mid-1740s most new bottles were square-shouldered cylinders and very different from those of the century's first decades. But did all bottles in use in the mid-eighteenth century reflect that evolution? To put it another way: Were old bottles discarded like outdated Coke bottles, or were they recycled and put back in service until broken or uncleanably fouled?

Hogarth's earliest bottle was a prop in his satire on the dumbing down of the English theater, but the bottle was French rather than English. It came encased in straw or wicker for it had no shaped foot of its own. Others from Flanders were intended to be tied by leather thongs to saddles and were securely wrapped in sewn canvas and laced with leather. Either way, the glass was weak and rarely has survived intact.

There were plenty of these "wanded" bottles on the mantle shelf and in the foreground of Hogarth's *A Midnight Modern Conversation*, a work of 1732, and another firmly clutched in the hand of a lady of the night in his orgy scene at the Rose Tavern in Drury Lane. This, plate III of his 1735 *Rake's Progress* series, shows several English-style bottles on the central table, none of them likely to date after about 1720. No later, and probably earlier, is another clearly drawn as overturned on the floor in *A Midnight Modern Conversation*.

In 1732 Hogarth and three artist friends made a trip from London to Rochester, the printed account of their travels ending with a tailpiece by Hogarth that included a bottle that could date anywhere from 1690 to 1720. There are as well a table fork and knife, the latter with a scimitar-shaped blade of a type which, though known, was scarce. So what should we conclude? Could it be that he was more interested in style than in substance?

Support for that likelihood is to be found in closer inspection of the drinking glasses on the Rose Tavern's cluttered table. The bowls of short-stemmed drinking glasses may not be round mouthed but six sided. Like the knife, such glasses did exist, but they are rare and so have become known to collectors as Hogarth glasses. The inference would seem to be that his affection for interesting shapes has resulted in his inadvertently transforming the really rare into the bogusly commonplace.

After almost twenty years of not drawing bottles, in 1755 Hogarth was again strewing a table with them—or, to be exact, two tables. Titled *An Election Entertainment,* the engraving shows two bottles with rings of torn paper hanging around their necks, one inscribed Champagne and the other Burgundy.

As a young slave to Hogarthian authenticity, I included similarly ringed bottles in the Raleigh Tavern scene of my Colonial Williamsburg film *Doorway to the Past.* But, of the *Election Entertainment* bottles, not one was of a shape that mirrored the standard

bottle's upward evolution in the mid-eighteenth century. Instead, the range of profiles was a reflection of Hogarth's earlier work and spanned the years from about 1700 to the 1740s. How come?

An answer, perhaps *the* answer, is that older bottles had longer lives than one might imagine. An illustration, below right, proves it. On the left is a bottle with a seal dated 1736. On the right is another that could be a few years earlier, yet its owner had engraved his initials and the date on its side: R.C. 1764.

That bottle was still in use the year that William Hogarth died and stands as proof that, like Norman Rockwell's, the eighteenth-century master's eye for detail should not glibly be doubted.

Hogarth's penultimate bottle dates from 1762 and features in his satire on superstition and credulity. In it, an old woman bootblack clutches a very large bottle whose cork has blown out to release a ghostly spirit to counteract the spells of witchcraft. In the drawing the woman is vomiting bent pins and nails—standard components in formulae for reverse magic.

But the bottle is much larger than any known witch bottle, though such half-gallon sizes existed. Should we conclude that Hogarth chose this unusual bottle, as he had the scimitar-shaped knife,

The post-election print of 1754, left, shows labeled wine and gin bottles of the 1720s and 1740s, as well as the results of overtoasting the winner. The next panel shows typical bottles of the 1730s, the one on the right still in use and engraved in 1764.

Throughout his career, Hogarth's treatment of bottles focused on those of the 1720s, like the one at left, perhaps because he derived no aesthetic pleasure from shapes in general use by 1760, like those at right, all from the author's collections.

because it was more important to make his point than to draw accurately a type that was used for a witch bottle?

He would draw his last bottle in the spring of 1764, and, like those he had depicted so often, its shape put it no later than about 1740.

All this seems to raise questions about the reliability of Hogarth's engravings as gospel-pure renditions of eighteenth-century objects. If he was wrong about his bottles, what else was not right?

There is no doubt that his brick walls sometimes lack the telltale coursing of English or Flemish bond, and no doubt, if one were a student of, say, fireplace hardware, as I have been of bottles, inconsistencies and inaccuracies could be cataloged and analyzed.

It is after all, the warp and weft of art appreciation or deprecation to seize on details of no importance to the whole or to find an allegory where none was intended. This Hogarth well knew when he satirized us in his drawing of a monkey watering a dead tree while examining it through a magnifying glass "to draw forth hidden beauties, which to *common optics* are invisible."

Those were the words of Hogarth's biographer John Ireland and are worth remembering whenever we presume to treat Hogarth's works of art as Sears catalogs of the eighteenth century.

In a detail from Credulity, Superstition and Fanaticism, *1762, Hogarth presented a bootblack vomiting bent pins and needles while clutching a 1730s witch bottle. His satirical engraving, below, cautions against reading too much into old pictures.*

German stoneware chamber pots were reaching Virginia by 1630. An example dated 1632 is decorated with a Germanic double-headed eagle, the same ornament that in 1803 English cartoonist James Gillray placed beneath the chair of a gluttonous foreign visitor.

Following the death of Virginia governor Lord Botetourt in 1770, the inventory of his valuables shipped home to England included one silver chamber pot. This example in the Colonial Williamsburg collection was made early in 1744.

Mentioning the Unmentionable

England's premier collector of German stone-wares pointed disdainfully to two blue-on-gray vessels isolated on a lower shelf of his vast collection and said, "You can have these. I don't want them." Frank Thomas's interests focused on the quality of the Rhenish wares and the artistry of the potters who made them. The disparaged pair had been part of a larger lot auctioned at Sotheby's, and Frank found their continuing presence offensive. His was what we now know as a decorative arts approach, whereas mine was that of a student of the human condition. The pots in question belonged *sub rosa*—or rather concealed under Rosa's bed. In short, chamber pots have long been the butt of indelicate jokes.

Nevertheless, it seems reasonable to assume that in the days before we had indoor plumbing these vessels were as much a part of contemporary life as mugs, bottles, or dishes. But reasonable assumptions can be far removed from historical reality. After several years of chamber pot contemplation, I have reason to conclude that in eighteenth-century Virginia they were not as proportionately represented as one might suppose necessary.

First, however, we need to get past what remains of Victorian prudery and propriety and think of these essential vessels in the same way that we can a teapot or a soup tureen. To begin at the apex of Elizabethan society, it is documented that when Queen Elizabeth I's household plate was cataloged it included a round basin and ewer "wth a pisspot of Silvr weighg 57. Oz." Several other now-obsolete names were also used, the most common being a "jordan" or a "looking glass." In seventeenth-century

In the eighteenth and nineteenth centuries earthenware chamber pots made ideal color dispensers for house painters and scenic artists, as the 1738 detail from William Hogarth's Strolling Actresses Dressing in a Barn *attests.*

inventories the latter leaves us uncertain whether the recorder was looking under a bed or at the reflection of his face. The answer in some instances was neither. A looking glass often meant a medical inspection glass, as clearly was the case in the Accomac County, Virginia, 1644 inventory of the late Phillip Chapman, which listed together a "Looking glass and a Chamber pott" worth sixty pounds of tobacco. By the eighteenth century, "chamber pot" had become the term of choice in Virginia—as it had in England.

In 1699 the completed and in-production stock of the London delftware factory known as the Pickleherring Pothouse was inventoried after the death of its manager, John Robins. It listed in excess of 3,000 chamber pots, numerically one of the largest single items in the lists. But what, I asked myself, did this mean in terms of household usage? How many pots might a London home have possessed at a time?

The population of the city in 1650 is thought to have been about 350,000 and had grown to approximately 600,000 by the end of the century. If we assume one dwelling to every eight people—75,000 homes—and that the eight persons in each house comprised a master, his wife, two children, and four servants, and that four chamber pots would not be an unreasonable number to serve them, we wind up with 300,000 pots concurrently in use in the city in the year 1700. At about that date a successful potter working at Hackney, north of London, made so much profit from the sale of these domestic necessities that he built himself a fine house that became known in the neighborhood as Piss Pot Hall.

With that as background, we turn to the only pre-1750 Virginia potter's inventory and find a startlingly different set of figures. The archaeological discovery of large quantities of waste and spoiled products from the earthenware and stoneware factory of William Rogers at Yorktown has prompted historians to charge Lieutenant Governor William Gooch with deliberately underplaying the level of Rogers's production. Throughout the eighteenth century there were laws on the books in England forbidding the colonial manufacture of anything that might have a detrimental impact on British exports. Consequently, Gooch's reports to the Lords of Trade referring to Rogers as the Poor Potter and his productivity as so very inconsiderable that it had no impact on importations from England are seen as a cover-up. So, too, was Gooch's assurance that

Rogers's product was the kind of lowly earthenware that only the poorest families would buy. The governor said as well that these were the kind of people who would do without if they had no opportunity to buy pots locally made.

Reading the inventory made at Rogers's death in 1739, and using the thirty-year-old Pickleherring stock as our yardstick, the Yorktown pottery's volume seems meager. Against John Robins's 3,000 chamber pots Rogers had 6. Nevertheless, the low number is supported by excavations on the factory site where the shard count identified chamber pots, stone and earthenware, as 0.756% of the total recovered. The value of Rogers's stock, in modern dollars, came to $35,306.72 compared with Robins's $112,780.08. So what does this tell us about the marketability of and, indeed, use of chamber pots in the Williamsburg area? Since that was not the kind of information that most householders thought worthy of inclusion in their diaries or in letters to their friends, we have the few surviving probate inventories on which to rely. At best, they

Williamsburg's self-documenting chamber pot. Found on the site of the 1770 Public Hospital, this white-ware pot of circa 1849 was made to order in England for the Williamsburg Lunatic Hospital.

A field guide to colonial-era chamber pots: (1–3) English, circa 1660, 1720, and 1740, (4) English delftware, circa 1720, (5) German stoneware pots standard and small, the latter with brass lid, circa 1730, (6) a Native American earthenware copy of the delft shape, found in a drain at the John Custis House in Williamsburg, circa 1740–70, (7) English white salt-glazed stoneware, circa 1760.

tell the York County part of the story, the records of James City County having been destroyed in Richmond during the Civil War. The Accomac and Northampton County records, begun in 1632, go back much further. In 1638 the Widow Roach's estate included "a mean bed with indifferent white rug, 1 very ragged sheet, a pillow bear and 1 old pewter piss pot." The pillow bear in the inventory is what we would call a pillowcase.

Pewter in every shape seems to have been more common in the mid-seventeenth century than in later years. Thus, an entry in the 1643 inventory of Northampton County resident John Holloway listed "4 saucers 6 porringers 16 pewter dishes & Chamber pott." Two years later, the wealthy William Burdett left, amid much-used and dented pewter, four pewter chamber pots worth sixty pounds of tobacco.

Few seventeenth-century pewter chamber pots survive, and most of those have been recovered from excavations in less than pristine state. I should add that they have rarely been put on display in museums, not because of their condition but for fear that they would engender unseemly comments from small children that might embarrass their parents. The Winthrop Rockefeller Archaeology Museum at Colonial Williamsburg's Carter's Grove breaks with that tradition and exhibits what I believe to be the earliest datable, Virginia-made earthenware chamber pot. We found it in a well of the fort in the settlement called Martin's Hundred abandoned around the time of the Indian attack in March 1622. Several more locally made chamber pots were found on the sites of slightly later homes, strongly suggesting that, for Martin's Hundred potter Thomas Ward, chamber pots had a ready market.

The Carter's Grove museum also displays a fragment of what is certainly the oldest stoneware chamber pot yet found in America. Made in the German Rhineland no later than about 1640, this plain brown pot has little visual appeal; but it stood at the dawn of a German export trade in stoneware chamber pots that would continue in England into the 1780s and into her American colonies until the onset of the Great Disagreement.

The earliest decorated German exports came from the Westerwald district of the Rhineland and carry dates from 1632 to 1677. An example of the former proudly displays a German two-headed eagle.

By 1700 the Westerwald exports had settled into a routine shape that persisted for about eighty years, and it was two of those that stoneware purist Frank Thomas chose to expel from his collection. Examples decorated with lions flanking stamped rosettes were by far the most common. There was another, however, that substituted molded, bull's-eye devices with hatched centers, a type represented by one of the two from the Thomas collection. I recalled no other like it until a child's size example found in Amsterdam was being auctioned on eBay, nor had I ever seen or heard of a Westerwald chamber pot of that size—or one that came with a lid. But this one did. The ever-helpful William Hogarth, however, included in his *Marriage à la Mode* a collection of auctioned rarities, among them a small chamber pot with an elaborate ceramic lid that I took to be of porcelain.

A portrait of Hogarth at his easel by artist John Mortimer included another such pot; but lying across it are two paintbrushes clearly showing that it was being used as a container for color. Full-sized, red earthenware pots were commonly used by house or theatrical scenery painters—as Hogarth shows in his 1738 engraving titled *Strolling Actresses Dressing in a Barn*. Two Westerwald pots we found on Williamsburg's Anthony Hay Cabinet Shop site contained white lead and black paint—which brings me to the documentary evidence for chamber pot usage in the eighteenth-century city.

Fifty-four probate inventories between 1708 and 1812 yield a total of 101 chamber pots. Six were described as stone, which could mean Westerwald stoneware or English white salt-glazed stoneware. Eight in 1748 were white, which could have been delftware but by the mid-century was more likely to be white salt-glaze. Two were of pewter and one of silver. This last had belonged to Lord Botetourt, and in 1771 it was shipped back to England with his effects. The remaining eighty-four were listed as earthenware or not described at all.

Although 101 pots may seem like a lot, it becomes modest when one finds that sixty were owned by five tavernkeepers and that ten more belonged to Philip Ludwell of nearby Green Spring

Plantation. That leaves thirty-one to be spread among forty-eight households, twenty-four of which had none at all. The explanation may be that vessels not made or shaped for the purpose were put into service in the poorer households, though not all the pot-challenged residences were otherwise impoverished. Ordinary-keeper Jean Marot, a substantial property owner, left an estate in 1717 worth £904.11.1—about $107,946.64 at today's exchange rate; Marot had no chamber pots but did own "1 close stool, 1 bed pan & 4 pales [pails]" together worth a modern $89.50.

Even if we take into consideration that, in its heyday, pre-Revolutionary Williamsburg had a permanent population of about 2,000 inhabitants, white and black, and recognizing that in the absence of the James City County Court records the studied inventories are but a sampling, we are still left with a puzzling shortage of documented cham-

ber pots. Under such circumstances we might suppose the slave population did without, but archaeology suggests otherwise.

A hand-shaped chamber pot copying a delft-ware form made on one of the Native American reservations was found inside a brick drain on the home site of Williamsburg's wealthy John Custis. Being so inferior to even the coarsest European earthenwares, such a pot was unlikely to have been acceptable even to the poor folks who Governor Gooch said would go without rather than pay the price for imported goods. The obvious inference, therefore, seems to be that the disenfranchised Virginia Indians were making cheap copies of English chamber pots and tableware for masters to supply to their slaves.

Of this there can be no doubt: we still have much to learn about the private side of life in colonial Virginia.

In my lady's chamber, her pot falls vitim to events.

A jumble of seventeenth- and eighteenth-century pipes. Though identical to others excavated at Jamestown and Williamsburg, these were found in London.

Hunting for a Little Ladle

The pipe, so lily-like and weak,
Does thus thy mortal soul bespeak.
—Rev. Ralph Erskine,
Gospel Sonnets *(ca. 1733)*

Throughout Virginia's colonial centuries, tobacco was the economic lifeblood of the Old Dominion, and, unless one rolled it to smoke as a cigar, or took it as snuff, a pipe was as necessary to its consumption as fire. Pipes are known in silver, brass, pewter, iron, and even lead, but clay was the primary material and so remained until the end of the nineteenth century. The clay pipes' fragility ensured that they were broken almost as fast as they were made, and fragments are strewn across every Virginia colonial home site. But, just as few of us give much thought to what later generations might deduce from our discarded bottle caps, no one in the eighteenth century considered how a twenty-first-century archaeologist might use his broken pipe as a clue to his life and time. Especially time. The characteristics of tobacco pipes changed with the years, and, if an archaeologist can date those changes, so can he date the objects with which they are found.

There are thousands of pipe fragments found in Williamsburg. An early explanation for their ubiquity had it that in colonial-era taverns pipes passed from mouth to mouth, but that in the interests of hygiene the previously lip-gripped section was broken off and thrown away. There is no documentary support for that notion, but it is known that used pipes were placed in iron cradles and heat cleansed in bake ovens before being issued to the next round of smokers.

The real explanation for the ubiquitous pipe-stem fragments is more prosaic: they were easily

The author holds a long clay "churchwarden" pipe, which is among the most fragile of eighteenth-century artifacts.

broken. If you drop a typical seventeenth-century eleven-inch clay pipe—something that curators try to avoid—its stem is likely to fracture into six or seven pieces, and, when you do the same for a long "churchwarden" pipe from the end of the eighteenth century, the fragments may run to as many as twenty. That all these little pieces might have something to say to archaeologists was first recognized in the mid-twentieth century when the National Park Service's archaeologist at Jamestown, Virginia, Jean Carl "Pinky" Harrington started studying not the stem fragments per se but the sizes of the holes through them.

By itself, this sounds like a lunatic occupation, and at the outset critics were quick to say so. Interest in the history of the evolution of the clay pipe's *bowl*, however, goes back a deal further and was the subject of scholarly interest as early as 1863.

In that year a clergyman named Hume, no relation to me, began an essay on the topic by saying that "very small pipes are found all over these islands, which are known in Ireland as Fairy pipes or Danes' pipes." The pragmatic cleric was quick to add that "the Irish attribute any thing unusually small to the fairies, and anything very ancient or inexplicable to the Danes." Nevertheless, it was true that the most ancient of pipes were, indeed, very small. The question, of course, was *how* ancient?

Conventional wisdom—at least that to be found in the pages of the *Encyclopaedia Britannica*—credits the introduction of the tobacco pipe to Europe to "Ralph Lane, first governor of Virginia, who in 1586 brought an Indian pipe to Sir Walter Raleigh and taught the courtier how to use it." The Reverend Hume thought so, too, asserting that the use of American tobacco began in England around 1585. If one wishes to narrow the source down to a few square yards, it is to be found at the National Park Service's Fort Ralegh on North Carolina's Roanoke Island. On that site we found fragments of Indian tobacco pipes smoked by the colonists who were there in 1585 and 1586.

Among them was Sir Walter Ralegh's protégé, Thomas Harriot, who on his return to England, wrote:

> We ourselves during the time were there used to suck it after their maner, as also since our returne, & have found maine rare and wonderful experiments of the vertues thereof . . . the use of it by so maine of late, men & women of great calling as else, and some learned Phisitions also, is sufficient witnes.

Harriot described the Indians' practice of "sucking it through pipes made of claie into their stomacke and heade; from which it purges superfluous steame & other grosse humors."

Like so much else in historical lore, the encyclopedia and the Reverend Hume were wrong. The Spaniards had known of the alleged benefits of tobacco smoking for close on a hundred years, having discovered its use from the conquered Indians of Central America. It was also known to the French in Florida long before Ralph Lane built his fort on Roanoke Island. Reporting on Sir John Hawkins's voyage to the West Indies in 1565, chronicler John Sparke wrote:

> The Floridians when they travell, have a kind of herbe dried, who with a cane and an earthen cup in the end, with fire, and the dried herbs put together, doe sucke thorow the cane the smoke thereof, which smoke satisfieth their hunger, and therewith they live foure or five dayes without meat or drinke, and this all the Frenchmen used for this purpose.

Whether it was Hawkins and not Ralegh who introduced pipe smoking to England or some passing Frenchman, there is no doubt that eight years after Hawkins's voyage, "taking in the smoke of the Indian herb called tobacco by an instrument formed like a little ladle . . . is greatly taken up and used in England." So here we have two descriptions of tobacco pipes that precede the Roanoke voyages, the first a cup attached to a cane, and the second shaped like a little ladle.

The first reference is to something resembling the typical American pipe of the nineteenth century, one that had come to North Carolina with Germanic immigrants in the middle of the previous century. At that time Moravian potters at Bethabara were making clay pipe bowls in designs that included the feather-capped human heads that might or might

Gunsmith Richard Frazier uses a taper to light a later version, with larger bowl and longer stem.

Elizabethans called a pipe a "little Ladell."

not have been intended to resemble Indians. An example of this cane-and-clay style in my collection is amusingly anachronistic, having been made as a souvenir of the Jamestown Exposition in 1907, its bowl shaped to resemble the island's ruined church tower. No such combination was used at the settlement in the seventeenth century.

By the time the first colonists landed at Jamestown, the English already had thirty years in which to develop their own tobacco pipe technology. A disapproving German visiting in 1598 noted that the "English are constantly smoking tobacco adding that they have pipes on purpose made of clay." No archaeologist has found such a pipe in a context that can be dated with any certainty prior to about 1600. A pipe found on the foreshore of the River Thames at London may be as close as we can yet come to 1573's little ladle. Unfortunately, it does not follow that tiny pipe bowls fit for fairies are necessarily older than others that are larger. The smallest yet found in Virginia were discovered in a context of 1622 beside the River James at Martin's Hundred, near Williamsburg.

Nineteenth-century interest in the age of pipes and their shapes was purely antiquarian. No one thought that they might be of use to archaeologists. In truth, Victorian-era archaeologists had no interest in anything from the seventeenth and eighteenth centuries. Nevertheless, antiquaries like the

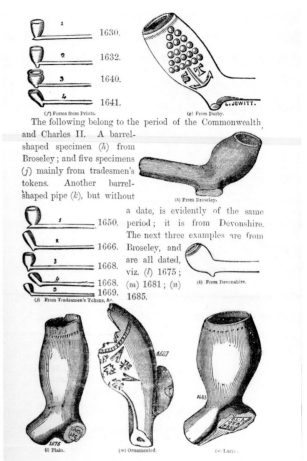

Antiquaries of the 1860s attempted to date clay pipe bowls by their evolving shapes and sizes. Few makers included dates in their marks, however.

An unexpected use for broken pipes. More than 4,000 fragments were made use of in this circa 1740 walkway beside Colonial Williamsburg's George Reid House on Duke of Gloucester Street.

Reverend Hume picked up pipe bowls in their gardens and wondered how old they were and why they differed in shape.

Finding any answer, not necessarily *the* answer, wasn't easy. Unlike the seventeenth-century Dutch, whose artists painted virtually every aspect of contemporary life—including smokers—British artists found their markets as portrait painters, none of whose sitters posed smoking. But there were minute pictures of tobacco pipes stamped onto tobacconists' trade tokens. In most instances these emblems were miniature versions of the signs hanging over the doors of their establishments. Thus, for example, in the village of Eton in 1666, tobacconist Richard Robinson issued a token showing his sign depicting two pipes crossed. Someone, perhaps it was the Reverend Hume, came up with the idea of drawing all the more than forty pipes so depicted. But, as an illustration from the reverend's book reveals, the exercise got him nowhere. Copies from earlier seventeenth-century engravings and woodcuts were no more informative. Pipes were an accessory, and, as long as they were shown having a stem with some sort of bowl on the end, the viewer got the idea.

Although the guild of tobacco pipe makers had been established in London as early as 1619, prompting makers to identify their products by inscribing their marks or initials on the bases of bowls, very few of them supplied a date. Most of those that did came from the pipe-making center at Brosley in Shropshire and were stamped with dates in the last quarter of the seventeenth century. As the bowls on which dates appeared varied in shape, and as the dates probably referred to the maker's acceptance into his guild and not to the pipes on which they appeared, all this evidence was as confusing as it was helpful.

More than eighty years would slip by before anyone else in England began to take an interest in clay pipes, and this time the clues were archaeological. From the slowly accumulated silting of the great ditch around the medieval city of London, which had been uncovered thanks to Hitler's bombing, came large numbers of seventeenth- and early eighteenth-century pipes. The then curator—they called him keeper—of the City's Guildhall Museum, Adrian Oswald, was the pioneer of postmedieval archaeology in England, and it was he who began to create a chronology of shapes on the basis of their location in the ground—those in the upper levels of the ditch being less old than those deeper down. If that sounds obvious, it is. All archaeological reasoning is firmly seated in common sense and is not nearly as abstruse as some practitioners might want you to believe.

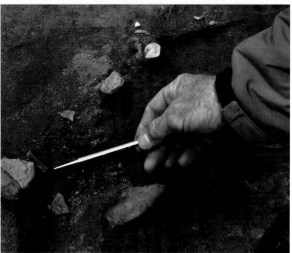

Top, in 1992, while searching for Sir Walter Raleigh's Lost Colony on Roanoke Island, North Carolina, excavators found fragments of aboriginal pipes smoked there by colonists in 1585 and 1586. From this small beginning the taste for "drinking tobacco" was born. Bottom, a pipe fragment found at Roanoke.

The author found this 1683 pipe in the River Thames. Makers often stamped their initials, though seldom on the bowl.

Oswald published his landmark findings in 1948, and immediately curators and archaeologists began to use his chronology. Quite independently, however, at Jamestown, where serious excavations had begun in 1933, National Park Service archaeologists were digging up pipes of many shapes and sizes and wondering what to make of them. One of the ponderers was anthropologist J. Somerfield Day, who seems to have been the first to suggest "that the wide range of pipe bowl shapes unearthed" at Jamestown "might provide an evolutionary series that could be used to distinguish different depositional dates." He was right.

Day's successor at Jamestown, Harrington, began by publishing an evolutionary series of shapes

The late Audrey Noël Hume had to measure the size of the hole through every one of the stem fragments from the George Reid House walkway.

akin to Oswald's, but he went further and began his sequencing by measuring the bores of the stem holes—big holes being early when the stems were short and decreasing in diameter as they were made longer and thinner. From that day onward, no self-respecting historical archaeologist has sallied forth without having at his disposal a set of wood drills graduated in sixty-fourths of an inch by which to measure the holes.

Harrington presented his sequencing in an easy-to-use chart showing the relative percentages of stem-hole sizes in five steps through the seventeenth and eighteenth centuries. That was in 1954. Almost immediately, Harrington's chart became the key to the grail. But how reliable was it?

As invariably happens, a mathematician, or nowadays a computer nerd, comes along to turn general trends into programmable numbers. In 1962, scholar Lewis Binford did just that, converting Harrington's modest progression into a math-

ematical formula that provided a mean or central deposition date for each assemblage of stem fragments. Nobody asked whether a mean date was really useful. But hailing it is as the DNA of historical archaeology, everyone used the formula—perhaps fearing that its neglect would be construed as not being on the cutting edge of the profession.

A year later, during Williamsburg excavations beside the Duke of Gloucester Street house occupied in the mid-eighteenth century by blacksmith Hugh Orr—today known as the George Reid House—we found a pathway paved with more than eleven thousand broken tobacco pipe fragments. Whether they represented a shipment that arrived shattered from England or had been discarded for some other reason, we never found out. But it was evident that they were related in time and origin, for many bore the same makers' marks. The late Audrey Noël Hume, in her role as archaeological curator, put the Binford formula through extensive testing and

Archaeologist Al Luckenbach, director of Maryland's Lost Towns Project, shows the author pipes and equipment found on a 1660s pipe maker's kiln site in Anne Arundel County. His is the most important contribution made to the history of colonial American pipe making.

found that to arrive at a consistent mean date required more than 1,000 fragments, a number much larger than is usually found together on a colonial site. In this case, however, 1,100 were sufficient to arrive at a consistent mean date of 1740—which was probably about right for that context.

Thirteen years later, during excavations at Martin's Hundred, the Binford formula got another body blow. Pipes from a single pit, all probably deposited at about the same time, gave Binford dates of 1619 and 1617 down to the lowest level at 1616. This would have been joyous news had not all the pipes been sitting on top of a slipware dish dated 1631.

With the pipe stem holes and bowl shapes analyzed to a fare-thee-well, one detail remained unquantified, namely the interior diameters of the bowls, which evidently were made larger as tobacco became cheaper. I resolved to base a new and all-revealing study of bowl mouths on examples recovered from tightly dated shipwrecks, mostly from Bermuda. The initial results were sufficiently encouraging to merit rehearsing the word *Eureka!* while shaving. But when I added much larger samplings from the no-less tightly dated Great Fire of London in 1666, my thesis turned to ashes.

Since Day, Harrington, and Oswald did their pioneering studies, more ink has been devoted to the dating of tobacco pipes than any other artifact category. A study of Bristol pipes alone ran to five thick volumes. The rolls of pipe makers' apprenticeships, bills, inventories, church and court records have been scoured to try to equate the names with initials on the pipes. Colonial Williamsburg's report on Martin's Hundred devoted forty-five pages to pipes and tried to separate one type from another, one date from another, and one manufacturing source from another—all the time blissfully unaware that buried beside a Maryland creek lay definitive answers to several of the questions.

In 1991, archaeologist Al Luckenbach discovered Emmanuel Drew's pipe-making factory site, active from 1661 to 1668, when a bulldozer scored the edge of a small hill and exposed artifacts that included a lump of burnt clay with fragments of tobacco pipe stems built into it. Drew's 1668 inventory listed "a payre of Brass Pype Moyldes"—the two-part molds used in shaping clay tobacco pipes.

There for the first time Luckenbach was seeing the scope of pipe-making designs and skills in a well-documented American context. The oldest tightly dated pipe-making site yet discovered, its fragments of kiln furniture, varieties of clays, and examples of the pipes themselves make this discovery of monumental importance to archaeologists on both sides of the Atlantic.

It also makes nonsense of many conclusions hitherto reached about the nationality or racial origins of contemporary pipe makers working in Virginia. Types that had been thought to be English made, weren't, and others believed to have been made only in Virginia were coming from Maryland.

Luckenbach's revelation made it crystal clear that an enormous amount has still to be learned about the history of tobacco pipes, and doubtless many more volumes to be published—none of them, one suspects, likely to make popular bedtime reading save as a substitute for counting sheep.

Top, from the Jamestown Exposition of 1909, pipes memorializing the settlement's ruined church tower. Middle, in the eighteenth century, smoked pipes were sanitized in iron cradles called kilns *and baked in ovens. Bottom, the stems of these English pipes from circa 1690–1720 measure eleven inches. The Dutch tobacco box is of the same period.*

In the morning light of Colonial Williamsburg's Governor's Palace kitchen window, historic foodways interpreter Dennis Cotner shucks fresh oysters.

An Oyster's Tale

*And all the little oysters
stood and waited in a row.*
—*Lewis Carroll,* Through
the Looking Glass

Nothing excites an archaeologist more than the sight of oyster shells glistening in the sunlight on a newly plowed field. It means the discovery of a *site*, a place where people lived and lunched perhaps hundreds, even thousands of years ago. Only closer inspection and the uncovering of other less light-reflecting clues can tell whether the people were Native American or Johnny-come-lately colonists. Oysters were a staple of the diet of both.

The first attempt at English colonization was in 1584 on Roanoke Island on the Outer Banks of what is now North Carolina. A year later, scientist Thomas Harriot surveyed the area's natural resources and found oysters "some very great, and some small; some round and some a long shape. They are found both in salt water and brackish, and those that we had out of salt water are far better than the other as in our country." When food became scarce, Governor Ralph Lane sent men to the mainland to live on oysters. Men did likewise at Jamestown, the first permanent English settlement in the New World, during the famishing winter of 1609–10.

Harriot noted that oysters had a secondary use which, in its way, was no less important. In the

151

Interpreter Emily James offers oysters for sale from a basket. Clamshells, like those at her feet, have replaced oyster shells on Williamsburg's walks.

Jamestown colonists ate when they landed in Virginia. On April 27, 1607, a reconnoitering party went ashore at Cape Henry, near modern Norfolk at the mouth of the Chesapeake Bay, where the Indians "had made a great fire, and had beene newly a rosting Oysters" but decamped when they saw the foreigners coming. Wrote gentleman George Percy, "We eat some of the Oysters, which were very large and delicate in taste."

Upstream, great solid banks of oysters protruded from the shallows, barely submerged at high tide. Writing about Lynnhaven Bay, Percy reported that mussels and oysters "lay on the ground as thick as stones. We opened some and found in many of them pearls." The Chesapeake pearls were of poor quality and worthless, but the idea of pearls being had for the taking was the kind of news that made the colony's London investors rub their hands in anticipation of treasure. For hungry Virginia settlers oysters meant food.

In 1612, colony secretary William Strachey said that the oysters were of the best and as much as

absence of limestone for making mortar, crushed oyster shells were an excellent substitute. And they were plentiful. "There is one shallowe sounde along the coast," he said, "where for the space of many miles together in length, & two or three miles breadth, the ground is nothing else." He compared the burning of shells for mortar as being "after the maner as they use in the Isles of Tenet and Shepy." These extended along the north coast of Kent and included the town of Whitstable, which, since Roman times, had been famous for its oyster beds, now destroyed by pollution and overfishing. Across the North Sea, the Dutch, too, had several uses for the oyster, one of them its inclusion in still-life paintings along with golden chalices and Chinese porcelain. Allegorically minded artists saw it as an invitation to sexual dalliance, and sometimes depicted it beside red-shelled lobsters, an imported rarity in seventeenth-century Holland, together symbolizing unwarranted and gluttonous wealth.

The oyster was the first indigenous fare the

Mendes da Costa's Elements of Conchology, *found in Thomas Jefferson's library, bristles with the Thorny Oyster, no. 4, and a fossil oyster, no. 2.*

thirteen inches in length. They had long been part of the Indians' diet from April through to the depths of winter. "The savages," Strachey wrote, "use to boil oysters and mussels together and with the broth they made a good spoon meat, thickened with the flour of their wheat and it is a great thrift and husbandry, with them to hang the oysters upon strings . . . and dried in the smoke, thereby to preserve them all the year." Then, as now, fishing in the James was a seasonal activity, the fish biting best in the spring and fall. Oysters, on the other hand, were always there for the taking. Wrote one colonist in 1623, "The most evident hope from altogether starving is oysters." Earlier in the frigid winter of 1609, which came to be known as "the starving time," at least sixty settlers were sent downriver from Jamestown to live on oysters. After nine weeks of that diet, one said, "This kind of feeding caused all our skin to peel off from head to foot as if we had been dead."

The Indians' ability to preserve oysters for future consumption had been demonstrated in the winter of 1607, when Captain John Smith and a foraging party lodged with them at Kecoughtan in modern Hampton. "The extreme wind, rain, frost, and snow caused us to keep Christmas among the savages," Smith wrote, "where we were never more merry, nor fed on more plenty of good oysters, fish, flesh, wild fowl, and good bread." On another occasion, Secretary John Pory recalled Indian leaders coming aboard his ship "with a brasse Kettle, as bright without as within, ful of boyled Oisters." But most of the references are to dried oysters. For example, colonists reported meeting two Indian women "with baskets full of dried oysters . . . and bartered with them for most of their victuals."

There is no detailed description of how the Indians prepared the oysters for drying beyond the statement that they roasted "their Fish and Flesh upon hurdells and reserve of the same untill the scarce tymes." Putting fish, and perhaps oysters, on spits, "they turne first the one syde, and then the other till yt be as dry as their Irkyn-beef . . . so they may keepe yt a moneth or more, without putryfying."

Although wading in the shallows for oysters in winter was not something to be gleefully under-

For a purpose unknown, oyster shells were packed between the floor joists of Pythian Castle in Portsmouth, Virginia.

taken, gathering them at the beginning of December in 1773 evidently was treated as an amusing expedition. On the thirteenth, Robert Carter III of Nomini Hall was reported to be "preparing for a Voyage in his Schooner, the *Hariot,* to the Eastern Shore in Maryland, for Oysters." With him were to go Colonel Richard Lee, Mr. Lancelot Lee, and another friend and neighbor, one Captain Walker, along "with sailors to work the vessel." Although nothing was said about the intended method of garnering the oysters, it was almost certainly by means of wood-handled iron tongs. It appears that the trip was abandoned when Walker was unable to go.

The value of the oyster for amusement is not appreciated today as it was in the eighteenth century, when *Chambers' Encyclopaedia* began its dissertation: "The oyster affords the curious in microscopic observations a very pleasing entertainment." Among the scientifically minded who thought so was Monsieur Joblot, who studied embryo oysters for several days and found them "swimming about nimbly and increasing in size daily," adding that "a mixture of wine, or the vapour of vinegar, killed them." He did not explain why he submitted them to either. Another scientifically inclined gentleman,

Mr. Lewenhoek, computed that "a hundred and twenty of them in a row would extend an inch."

When examined in the dark, oyster shells gave off a blue light, which the microscope showed was composed of three varieties of "animalcules." The first had "twenty-five legs on a side, forked, a black speck on one part of the head, the back like an eel with the skin stripped off." If that wasn't scary enough, the second variety was red, "resembled the common glow-worm with folds on its back, but legs like the former, a nose like a dog's, and one eye in the head." The third was larger and had "great heads, two horns like a snail, and six or eight whitish feet." Then there was the oyster worm discov-

A spat, a baby oyster, attaches itself to a mature shell.

At the Virginia Institute of Marine Science, oysters and a crab help re-create Chesapeake Bay life in an aquarium.

ered by Monsieur De Lavoye in 1666. He noted that, when "large and robust, they move their heads and tails about." Though "they are not apt to give light when irritated," when left to themselves, they emitted light that would glow for hours. At the Virginia Institute of Marine Science oyster specialist Bob Diaz has never seen the blue light, but he has identified three of the described intruders as the oyster mud worm, species *Polydora;* the clamworm, species *Nereis;* and another he defined only as a *nudibranch* species. Had eighteenth-century satirist Jonathan Swift been aware of these aliens within, he would have had even more reason to assert that "he was a bold man who first ate an oyster." Knowing all that, it is surprising that anyone risked eating oysters no matter whether there was an "R" in the month.

One assumes that apothecaries were unaware of the minimonsters lurking in the shells. Chambers said that oyster shells were "an alcali of a more powerful kind than is commonly supposed, and probably are in reality a much better medicine than many of the costly and pompous alcalis of the same class." All one had to do was grind them to powder in a mortar, let it dry in the sun, then pass it through a sieve. Taking twenty-five or thirty grains every morning for three weeks would have a salutary effect on stomachs "injured by acid humours."

Although today we tend to look on oysters as a delicacy and a luxury, the quantities readily available from the Chesapeake and southeast England in the eighteenth and nineteenth centuries rendered them as common and cheap as cockles or mussels. Women carried them in baskets to sell in the streets and taverns, having waited at dawn at London's Billingsgate fish market for the oyster boats to come in. So numerous were they that the wharf was known as Oyster Street. Writing in 1851, social historian Henry Mayhew described the scene:

> On looking down the line of tangled ropes and masts, it seems as though the little boats would sink with the crowds of men and women thronged together on their decks. . . . The red cap of the man in the hold bobs up and down as he rattles the shells about with his spade. These holds are filled with oysters—a grey mass of sand and shell.

Shells helped drainage in a 1770s tavern planting bed in Hampton, Virginia.

Then off went the costermongers, male and female, shouting, "Mussels, a penny a quart! Oysters, a penny a lot!"

A mid-eighteenth-century *Lady's Companion* gave eight recipes for a "Ragoo of Oysters," served as a second course, another to fricassee them, four ways to put them in a pie, two ways to make "Petit Patties," and another to prepare an "Oyster or Cockle Fraze." Isaac Welde, a visitor to Williamsburg in 1796, dined with the president of the College of William and Mary along with "half a dozen or more of the Students, the eldest about twelve years old" and was surprised to find "a Couple of Dishes of salted Meat, and some Oyster Soup, formed the Whole of the Dinner."

It seems likely that wealthy plantation owner William Byrd disliked oysters in any form. His daily journal recorded everything he ate, from roast rabbit to salt fish, but never mentioned oysters. Byrd's contemporary John Custis may or may not have been an oyster eater, but he was a shell collector, specimens of which he sent to his London friend Peter Collinson. If these included oysters, they undoubtedly came from the Miocene marl beds that underlie the Virginia's Middle Peninsula. In March 1740/41 Collinson said he did not know "which are those shells that was found so Deep when you were Makeing the Mill Dam."

Custis's elaborate Williamsburg gardens were interlaced with gravel walkways. Had he a copy of Richard Bradley's *Family Dictionary* of 1725 he might have covered the gravel with a layer of burnt oyster shells. "Constant rolling," Bradley said, "incorporates with the gravel, and prevents it sticking to ones Shoes." At Nomini Hall to the north, Robert Carter paved his walks with brick "covered over with burnt Oyster-Shells," a lone example of which practice was found during excavations of a seventeenth-century house site close by the much later Williamsburg Public Hospital.

In Hampton, between perhaps 1770 and 1780, a fifty-foot-long planting bed in a tavern yard was lined with oyster shells for drainage. Less easily explained was the packing of shells between the floor joists of an 1897 building in downtown Portsmouth, Virginia. Archaeologist David Hazzard, who photographed the phenomenon, has suggested that it may have been someone's idea of rodent control, wood preservation, or moisture protection. As Hazzard said, it's anyone's guess.

Using burnt shells for walkways or dumping them between floor joists was not oysters' primary residual function. As Thomas Harriot noted, in the absence of natural limestone, oyster shells were the colonial alternative to lime for mortar.

To produce "quicklime," one dug a conical hole in the region's natural clay and filled it with shells layered with firewood. Covered over with dirt, the wood was left to burn for hours. A 1734 *Builder's Dictionary* said the fire took away "all its Humidity, and opening its Pores, so that it becomes easily reduced to powder." A more refined form, "slak'd lime," was the product of washing the burnt shells in water. When dried, the resulting powder was packed into barrels to be carried to the building sites. To an archaeologist, the discovery of brickwork bonded with oyster-shell-flecked mortar is a clue as primal as a smoking gun, for it was not until the early nineteenth century that limestone

Tidewater oystermen, perhaps from the 1930s, in a hand-tinted photo.

brought from the hinterland was used in coastal construction.

A 1930s archaeologist working for Colonial Williamsburg put such store by the shell content of mortar that he carried around a partitioned box containing samples chipped from buildings of known date. He believed that, by comparing them with mortar he found in a buried foundation, he could determine when in the seventeenth or eighteenth century the foundation had been laid. We now know that this was nonsense. The size and quantity of shell fragments varied from one mortar batch to another. Indeed, the foundations of Williamsburg's Wetherburn's Tavern were laid with mortar mixed from at least three batches.

When modern Wetherburn's visitors see piles of oyster shells heaped between the outbuildings, they'll know that it's time for the lime burner's assistant to come round to collect them. That the piles never get smaller is because Colonial Williamsburg does not yet include lime making among its outdoor activities. Nevertheless, when in season, oysters may be on the menu at the King's Arms. The *Williamsburg Cookbook* offers six recipes for them, and the more recent *Favorite Meals from Williamsburg: A Menu Cookbook* five more.

Chesapeake oysters were plentiful during Virginia's early days, but they, like those days, are gone. In 1686 a French Huguenot visitor recalled that his host had no trouble obtaining as many oysters as he wanted. "He had only to send one of his servants

in one of the small boats," wrote Durand de Dauphine, "& two hours after ebb-tide he brought back full. These boats made of a single tree hollowed in the middle, can hold as many as fourteen people & twenty-five hundredweight of merchandise."

In 1858 another visitor said Newport News and Hampton were "in the very heart of oysterdom," whose "subacqueous metropolis of that luscious realm slumbers beneath our paddles." Not content with one purple passage, the writer added another: "In the waters surrounding Hampton Roads the marvelous mollusk hath its supreme court and citadel. *The* oyster does not exist elsewhere." He dismissed the English, Dutch, and French oysters "as an unsuccessful caricature of the animal . . . little, hard, black, and brassy."

Today, because of the overharvesting that began with the introduction of the steam canning process in the 1870s, coupled with two devastating parasitic diseases and increasing toxicity in the bay, the "Bounty of the Chesapeake" has dwindled to about 10 percent of the bushels being hauled a century ago. Public beds in Virginia are closed, and very few private beds are worked. Overfishing first by hand-hauled and later by mechanical dredges was the original culprit that destroyed the fragile shell beds to which the young oysters must adhere to survive. The late nineteenth century's ever-growing market for shucked and canned oysters, and the resulting diminution of local supplies, led to the importation of live oysters from the Gulf of Mexico.

The Gulf oysters brought with them the parasitic disease Dermo. If that were not mistake enough, in the 1950s rebuilding the beds with stock brought from the Pacific Northwest resulted in the arrival of another protozoan parasite, MSX. The diseases brought Chesapeake-region natural-bed oyster fishing to a halt.

Careful monitoring by the College of William and Mary's Virginia Institute of Marine Science (VIMS) and their research into the eradication of parasitic diseases are the best hope to prevent the Virginia oyster going the way of the passenger pigeon. In the meantime, VIMS scientists have embarked on a program to breed enough disease-free hatchlings to eventually refurbish newly primed beds in the York, James, and Rappahannock estuaries.

Highwaymen of the High Seas

"I have always abhorred such sort of profligate men and their barbarous actions; for such they are the disgrace of mankind."

—Governor Francis Nicholson

Fifteen men on the deadman's chest
Yo-ho-ho and a bottle of rum!
Drink and the devil had done for the rest—
Yo-ho-ho and a bottle of rum!
—Robert Louis Stevenson,
Treasure Island

Those of us who, as children, were thrilled by Stevenson's tale of high-seas derring-do or remember booing the malignantly comical Captain Hook in a production of J. M. Barrie's *Peter Pan* are likely to imagine the life of a pirate as enviable in its freedom and adventure. The idea of partying with assorted wenches while sitting on a chest filled with jewels and gold doubloons has

undeniable appeal. Alas, as every buccaneer well knew and as any reader of contemporary profiles of individual pirates can discover, being "on the account," as it was called, was a vocation no more glamorous than and no different from that of the highway murderer and common thief.

Coupled with dreams of swashbuckling adventure, our images are likely to be of sailing through azure seas amid the tropic isles of the Caribbean. That piracy could also be a cold, wet, and bloody business conducted in the forbidding gray waters of the North Atlantic has no place in our Technicolor-enriched imaginations. In truth, however, piracy was an ever-present menace throughout the history of the British American colonies. Indeed, from the outset of colonization, there were those who considered the Jamestown settlers no better than pirates in training.

In October 1607, only months after the colonists' arrival, Pedro de Zúñiga, Spain's ambassador in London, wrote to his king warning that the land in Virginia "is very sterile, and consequently there can be no other object in that place than it seems good for piracy, and that should not be permitted." Two years later Zúñiga was still banging the same drum. He accused the Virginia Company of appealing to James I to agree and command that "all the pirates who are out of this kingdom will be pardoned . . . if they resort there." Virginia, the ambassador insisted, is a place "so perfect for piratical excursions that Your Majesty [Philip III] will not be able to bring silver from the Indies without finding a very great obstacle there."

The reality, of course, was that the close-to-starving Virginia colonists had neither the strength nor the ships to go a-roving. At the same time, the recognition that Spain believed otherwise kept the colonists in constant fear of invasion. Although Zúñiga's warnings were unfounded, there could be no denying that English ships en route to Virginia often carried letters of marque permitting them to attack and loot vessels belonging to Britain's enemies. Under such authorizations, crews would sign on for Virginia-bound voyages with the expectation of being paid out of the profits of legalized piracy.

Once at sea, of course, it was impossible to know what treaties might have been signed or new enemies identified during the ship's absence. Consequently, the temptation to attack and apologize later was hard to resist. A classic example was provided in 1590 when the distraught John White was trying to raise a fleet to carry supplies to his colonists on Roanoke Island. He set out aboard the *Hopewell* along with three other ships, one of them commanded by Christopher Newport—later of Jamestown fame—and spent three months from April to July cruising the Caribbean in search of scarce victims before heading north to Virginia.

Elizabeth I and James I both secretly benefited from the success of British privateers, as, indeed, did private backers of westbound voyages. In 1618 the ship *Treasurer*, fitted out in London ostensibly for an American fishing trip, was "secretly armed as a man of war" and, through the good offices of the piratically inclined Earl of Warwick, her captain, Daniel Elfrid, was supplied with "an olde commission of hostility from the Duke of Savoy against the Spaniards." On reaching Jamestown the *Treasurer* was sent by Virginia's Governor Argall "rovinge in ye Spanish Dominions in the West Indies," augmenting its crew with some of the colony's most able men.

"Elated with their booty, they had nothing now to think of but some safe retreat where they might hive themselves up to all the pleasures that luxury and wantonness could bestow."
—Captain Charles Johnson, Lives of the Most Notorious Pirates

Although the details are unclear, it seems that the *Treasurer*'s mission included the obtaining of slaves and that the "20. And odd Negroes" later left at Jamestown from aboard a Dutch warship were part of the human cargo acquired by Captain Elfrid, the rest of whom he later offloaded at Bermuda.

The involvement of Governor Samuel Argall in aiding and promoting piracy for profit—as opposed to national interest—set an unholy precedent for government officials that would endure for decades, both in Virginia and North Carolina. Thus, for example, in 1680, when Captain Roger Jones came to Virginia with its new governor, Lord Culpeper, he was given the task of suppressing piracy in the Chesapeake Bay, an occupation that greatly enhanced Jones's personal fortune. Twelve years later, the Council of Virginia complained to the secretary of state, the Earl of Nottingham, that Jones had "learnt to cheat ye King very early" and that, instead of routing out the pirates, he was "adviseing, trading & sheltering severall Pyrates & unlawful Traders . . . by which means ye sd. Jones laid ye foundation of his p'sent great Estate."

The duplicitous Captain Jones had two sons who came to Virginia in 1702, one of whom occupied a part of that great estate, a tract located at Tutter's Neck, on land destined to be owned by Colonial Williamsburg. We excavated the remains of Frederick Jones's plantation house in 1960 and found fragments nearby of many wine bottles, several with glass seals impressed with his FI initials, prompting us to speculate as to the level of yo-ho-hoing that had gone on in the house where piracy was not a dirty word.

In 1708 or thereabouts, Jones moved to North Carolina. In 1717 he was appointed by Governor Robert Eden to be that colony's chief justice, replacing Tobias Knight, whose collusion with the most famous of all pirates, Edward "Blackbeard" Teach, was too blatant for even Governor Eden to ignore. Nevertheless, it was while Jones served as the colony's chief legal officer that Eden granted an ostensibly reformed Blackbeard and his crew the king's pardon. Having obtained a plantation in sight of the governor's own home, Teach settled into the life of a country gentleman and bigamously married the daughter of a local planter—

he reputedly had a dozen other wives—at a ceremony performed by Eden. There can be little doubt, therefore, that Williamsburg's Frederick Jones was on more than nodding terms with the most feared rover of them all.

Blackbeard was not only an unusually fearsome individual, but he also was operating on a far grander scale than the majority of pirates. His career had begun as companion to an old buccaneer named Benjamin Hornigold, whose base was in the Bahamas. Together they sailed up to the Virginia Capes, there careened their ships, then continued north in search of prey in the Delaware Bay. After a string of successes that took them back into the Caribbean, Hornigold retired, leaving his men and his ships to Teach, who soon fell in with another pirate, albeit one of an entirely different cut. Major Stede Bonnet was a respected gentleman from Barbados who decided to go pirating to get away from his wife. Being no more successful under the black flag, Major Bonnet's short and incompetent career ended in the Cape Fear River, when he was captured and later tried and hanged at Charleston along with forty-nine of his men.

When Blackbeard and Bonnet had audaciously tried to blockade the Charleston River, they had done so with a fleet of four large ships and a crew of as many as 700 buccaneers. They, however, represented the apex of piracy. At the other end—and much more common—were the small-time villains, who began their careers with a rowboat and four or five crewmen. Relying on surprise and often attacking moored vessels only slightly larger than their own, they rarely moved up into oceangoing piracy. Social misfits, escaped slaves, and indentured runaways, these men were frequently illiterate and inept seamen, whose successes were the product only of animal cunning and brute strength.

A little book published in 1755 entitled *The Travels of Mr. Drake Morris . . . Written By Himself* tells how he reluctantly became a pirate by joining a gang of eight men in a small boat, who together seized and transferred to larger vessels as their fortunes improved. The fruits of piracy were rarely as we like to imagine them, and this was particularly true of prizes seized in Virginia waters. Whereas the Spanish treasure *flotas* sailing through the Caribbean

The best of times and the worst of times—such was the pirate's lot. The bottle, opposite, was found at Tutter's Neck, above, the home of Frederick Jones and part of the estate and fortune his father had amassed through sheltering "several Pyrates & unlawful Traders."

could be expected to be laden with gold, silver, and jewels, as well as with the costly baggage of home-ward-bound grandees, Virginia voyagers often trav-eled with little more than trip money aboard ships whose holds held tobacco, lumber, hides, sassafras, and the like. None of this was intrinsically worth anything to the pirates until and unless they could find dishonest colonists willing to exchange the sto-len cargoes for cash.

Such, it would appear, were the kinds of deal-ings of which Roger Jones was accused and Edward Teach was able to develop with the reputable mer-chants of Bath town. After the capture of Black-beard's *Adventure,* the loot found aboard was by no means the stuff of romance: twenty-five barrels of sugar, eleven vats and 145 bags of cocoa, a barrel of indigo, and a single bale of cotton. The story of Blackbeard's return to piracy and his eventual death at the hands of Virginia's Lieutenant Maynard has been told too often to need repeating. Had he not been felled by twenty-seven cutlass wounds and five pistol balls, he would have been brought back to Virginia to stand trial in Williamsburg, as were

fifteen of his crewmen. They, however, were not the only pirates to contemplate their fate from the confines of Williamsburg's jail.

In 1727, the small-fry rover John Vidal—who had kept most of his petty piracy to the confines of the North Carolina sounds—and three accomplices, one of them a woman, were sent for trial before the Vice Admiralty Court in Williamsburg, where all but the woman were condemned to death. His-tory does not record whether the scratching of Vi-dal's quill kept his fellow prisoners' nerves on edge, but scratch it did—and to good effect. In a long and pusillanimous plea for mercy, he declared that he "never intended to go a pirating" and "with a weep-ing heart" begged the governor to "give me longer time of Repentance than the Rest." He was referring to his two companions who had already been ex-ecuted. Vidal wrote his letter on August 31, just be-fore the arrival of a new governor, Colonel William Gooch, and the timing could not have been better. Having sought the advice of his council, Gooch con-cluded that granting Vidal the king's clemency could be an appropriate act in honor of the accession of George II. Consequently, Vidal was freed.

Had the merciful governor known a week or two earlier that in September no fewer than seven Virginia-bound ships had been seized by a couple of Havana-based privateers within 100 miles of the Virginia coast, he might have been less ready to let Vidal go. The privateers were, as the term makes clear, privately operated vessels roving with the blessing of Spain to attack English ships, the two countries then being engaged in a final convulsion of the War of Spanish Succession that lasted from 1727 to 1729.

Throughout the colonial centuries and until the end of the Napoleonic era, Britain was involved, more or less continuously, in somebody's war. This, of course, suited freebooters of other nations quite admirably; for, armed with the authority of a Spanish, French, or Dutch permit, they were free to do their worst in the knowledge that if caught, they would not—or at least should not—be hanged as common pirates. Throughout those many years, Virginia's governors were compelled to spend much time and effort trying to keep the shipping lanes open and to have men-of-war constantly patrolling the coasts and bays in often futile efforts to keep the sea wolves from the commonwealth's door.

The apprehension of a pirate ship could endear a colonial governor to the planters and traders, who spent much of their time with fingers crossed in hopes of their cargoes' safe passage. In the fall of 1699, during the administration of Governor Francis Nicholson, Virginia merchants were loud in their complaints that the heavily armed pirate ship *Providence*, lying in wait at the mouth of the James River, had looted as many as thirty ships in the space of three months. The pirate captain, a Welshman named John James, was described by one of his victims as claiming to be the infamous Captain Kidd, whom Nicholson had orders to apprehend. James was reportedly "of middle stature, square-shouldered, large jointed, lean, much disfigured with the small-pox, broad [of] speech, thick-lipped, a blemish or cast in his left eye, but courteous." He may also have been prone to wild exaggeration, for he claimed to have £3,000,000 in gold and silver on board, an enormous sum in any age. James was not short of cash, as attested by the fact that, on capturing the ship *Maryland Merchant*, he allowed one of the passengers to retain valuables worth about £100.

Although James had first been challenged at the end of July, he was still plying his trade in Virginia waters in September. However, after outgunning Virginia's small coastal defense ship HMS *Essex*, and before a more formidable navy ship could arrive, James departed with his loot intact.

In the following April, another pirate ship, a large French vessel named *La Paix* with a 140-man crew, lay off Virginia's Lynnhaven Bay, plundering any ship that came its way. No doubt embarrassed by the previous year's failures, Governor Nicholson allegedly decided to personally take charge of the navy's response. He boarded the British man-of-war *Shoreham* in Hampton Roads and, with her captain at his side, engaged the *La Paix* in a five-hour battle that ended with the pirate ship running aground and surrendering. Not surprisingly, this adventure gave the governor "much Credit with those, who rely'd on his own Account of the Matter." So wrote Robert Beverley, a contemporary Virginia historian whose dislike of Nicholson was no secret. According to Beverley, Captain Passenger, commander of the *Shoreham*, took offense and declared "that no Body had pretended to command in that Engagement but himself" and went on to challenge Nicholson to

Gentleman Stede Bonnet, one of history's most incompetent pirates, paid the price for his ungentlemanly behavior at Charleston on November 10, 1718.

state "whether he had given the least Word of Command all that Day, or directed any one thing during the whole Fight." Beverley added that "his Excellency tamely acknowledged that what the Captain said was true." Passenger alone deserved the honor of victory.

Today, the presence of a state governor sailing into action aboard a U.S. Coast Guard ship would probably be dismissed as a cynically motivated photo opportunity. Indeed, in a self-promotional sense, Governor Nicholson's presence on the *Shoreham* may have been, and probably was, just that. Thus, the different spins on the affair of *La Paix* serve as a reminder that history is based largely on such information as happens to survive and that, when the waters are muddied by two different accounts coming down to us, acceptance of one or the other and our interpretation of it can be dependent on our own biases.

Just as John James and his *Providence* had sailed away and out of the pages of recorded history, so most of the buccaneers who served under the black flag left no lasting record of their exploits. Nevertheless, a few—by their audacity or by the accident of getting caught—have found their way into legend. Teach, Kidd, Avery, Bellamy, Bonnet, and Lafitte, as well as the brief careers of female pirates Anne Bonney and Mary Read, are names carved deep in the sands of time. So, too, is the belief that from the shores of New York to the islands of the Indies there still lie buried chests of loot that pirates known and unknown never had the opportunity to retrieve. Alas, no X-marked maps have been found to point to a Virginia treasure site, but, if a Gloucester tale is to be believed, an anonymous somebody did know where to look.

At the end of the nineteenth century—or it may have been in the first years of the twentieth—a yacht registered in New York is said to have dropped anchor in the York River not far from the Page family home at Rosewell. Local residents wondered why it was there, but they made no contact with its crew. Dawn of the next day found the yacht gone, leaving behind a large hole at the top of the tidal shore and in it the red-rust impression of an ironbound chest—but traces of neither fifteen men nor a bottle of rum.

IMAGE CREDITS

The author and publisher wish to thank the following museums, libraries, institutions, companies, and individuals for permitting the reproduction of works of art or photographs in their possession.

"The Great American Incognitum"
Hessisches Landesmuseum Darmstadt: x
The Maryland Historical Society, Baltimore, Maryland: 3
Collection of The New-York Historical Society, 8736, 1940.202: 4
American Philosophical Society: 5
The Library Company of Philadelphia: 6

"Jamestown Revisited"
Image Alchemy: 16, 17, 18, 19

"Message from Maine"
Collections of Maine Historical Society, No. 7542: 22, 24 (right), 25 (left)
National Portrait Gallery, London: 23 (bottom right)

"St. Mary's City"
Image courtesy of Historic St. Mary's City: 35

"Louisbourg"
Louisbourg: A Living History by Susan Biagi, Formac Publishing Company Limited: 46
Lewis Parker; Parks Canada: 48 (top)

"Witchcraft and Evil Spirits"
Image Alchemy: 91

"Sir Francis and the Phantom Chicken"
Detail from Francis Bacon, Viscount St. Alban, NPG 1288, National Portrait Gallery,
    London: 101
Nathan Nice: 104

"A Window on Williamsburg"
Bermuda Archives, P.A. 605: 108–109

"A Plague Profiteer?"
Museum of London: 115, 117

"An Oyster's Tale"
David K. Hazzard: 153
Courtesy of the Hampton History Museum: 155

"Highwaymen of the High Seas"
Colonel Charles Waterhouse: 157, 158
Richard Stinely: 160